650

Ireland
A DIVIDED ISLAND

TONY REA
AND JOHN WRIGHT

OXFORD UNIVERSITY PRESS

Oxford University Press,
Great Clarendon Street, Oxford OX2 6DP

Oxford New York

*Athens Auckland Bangkok Bogota Bombay
Buenos Aires Calcutta Cape Town Dar es Salaam
Delhi Florence Hong Kong Istanbul Karachi
Kuala Lumpur Madras Madrid Melbourne
Mexico City Nairobi Paris Singapore
Taipei Tokyo Toronto Warsaw*

and associated companies in
Berlin Ibadan

Oxford is a trade mark of Oxford University Press

Printed in Italy

The authors would like to thank Peter Allott for his help in
researching part of the text.

The authors would like to thank Mark Byrne for making
available Source E on page 63.

*The publishers would like to thank the following for
permission to reproduce photographs:*

Belfast Telegraph: p 41; British Library: p 5;
Camera Press: pp 36 (top), 43 (bottom), 48;
Camera Press/J Gray: p 67 (top); Camera Press/Jane
Furmanovsky: p 64 (bottom left); Centre for the
Study of Cartoons and Caricature, University of
Kent/JAK: p 66/67; Centre for the Study of
Cartoons and Caricature, University of
Kent/Trog/The Observer: p 44 (bottom); Corbis UK
Ltd: pp 4, 21 (left), 63, 76 (bottom right);
Corbis/Bettmann/UPI: pp 26, 40; Corbis UK
Ltd/Leif Skoogfors: p 59 (bottom); Crawford Art
Gallery, Cork: p 33 (top); , e.t. Archive: p 6; e.t.
Archive/Tate Gallery: p 7; Mary Evans Picture
Library: p 13; Eye Ubiquitous/Paul Seheult: pp 55,
64 (top), 64 (bottom right), 65 (top); Getty
Pictures/Hulton Picture Library: pp 11 (top), 18,
21 (right), 30, 31, 35, 44 (top), 46, 52 (left), 62
(top), 76 (left); Imperial War Museum: pp 19, 25,
61; The Kobal Collection: p 33 (bottom);Library of
Congress: p 16 (top); Magnum/Luc Delahaye: pp
74, 75; Magnum/Don McCullin: p 45; Sidney
Matchett: p 49; National Library of Ireland: p 66
(left); National Museum of Ireland: pp 22, 24;
Network: pp 53, 56 (top); Pacemaker/William
Cherry: p 4; Popperfoto: pp 9, 43 (top), 54 (bot-
tom), 56 (bottom), 65 (bottom);
Popperfoto/Associated Press: p 77 (left);
Popperfoto/Reuters/Kieran Doherty: p 76 (top
right); Popperfoto/Reuters/Crispin Rodwell: pp 68,
72; Popperfoto/Reuters/Ian Waldie: p 71 (both);
Popperfoto/UPI/G Kemper: p 54 (top); Press
Association/Neil Munns: p 59 (top); Press
Association/Michael Stephens: p 73; Public Record
Office of Northern Ireland/The Deputy Keeper of
the Records: p 12 (top); Punch Library and Archive:
p 11 (bottom); Royal Ulster Constabnlary: p 28;
Topham Picture Library: pp 16 (top), 23, 36 (bot-
tom), 52 (top right), 57, 77 (right); Topham Picture
Library/Associated Press: p 62 (bottom)Topham
Picture Library/Press Association: pp 52 (bottom
right), 58, 70; Topham Picture Library/Press
Association/John Giles: p 51;

The publishers have made every effort to trace the
copyright holders of all photographs, but in some
cases have been unable to do so. They would
welcome any information which would enable them
to rectify this.

Designed by Peter Tucker, Holbrook Design
Oxford Ltd

Maps by Jeff Edwards

Illustrations and diagrams by Peter Tucker

Contents

Preface

This book has been written specifically for students using Ireland as a Modern World Study as part of their SHP History syllabus at GCSE. It covers all of the GCSE objectives, and includes a comprehensive background to the Northern Ireland issue from the first attempts at conquest by the British to the present day.

A large number of primary and secondary sources are integrated with the detailed and strongly narrative text. Maps, diagrams and photographs both enliven the text and enhance the students' understanding of it. The book is also supplemented by biographies of key individuals and 'features' which enable students to reflect upon the narrative and consolidate their learning. These lively pages encourage students to re-read and process the text, as well as presenting them with challenging and structured tasks. The 'features' focus upon evidence skills as well as historical concepts and so can be used as coursework assignments for GCSE, or as 'dry run' assignments with which to prepare students.

At the back of the book are two blank pages. These are 'update pages' which, in future editions, will be filled with post 1997 developments in Northern Ireland. In this edition, however, teachers might like to encourage their students to select newspaper clippings of recent developments which can then be glued into the update pages or kept in a separate file.

1 The coming of the English, 1169–1690

A

Tony Blair being jostled by angry Unionists in October 1997, after it became known that he had shaken hands with Gerry Adams of Sinn Fein

In September and October 1997, there was great optimism that solutions could be found to the problems in Northern Ireland. Leaders of the Ulster Unionists and Sinn Fein met for the first time in more than 50 years. Tony Blair, Prime Minister of Great Britain and Northern Ireland, made an historic visit to Belfast, where he met and shook hands with Gerry Adams, one of the leaders of Sinn Fein; and in December Adams went to Downing Street for talks with Blair. The Secretary of State for Northern Ireland, Mo Mowlam, said that if all sides were prepared to talk to each other, then the hopes for reaching a settlement were not unfounded.

Why are Ireland and Northern Ireland so much a part of our political scene today? The roots of the conflict are to be found in the past, and it is difficult to know where to select a starting point. This book has taken the twelfth century, when King Henry II of England (1154–1189) sent an army to conquer Ireland.

Henry II to William of Orange

Henry II invaded in 1169. He had been given permission by Pope Adrian IV, who wished to see the Irish crushed because they were developing their own form of Roman Catholicism. Adrian was happy to see Ireland under English military control, provided that the Irish stayed under his religious control.

The invasion was not a success. The English could only secure control of an area around Dublin known as The Pale. Nevertheless, Henry still considered himself Lord of Ireland. In the following centuries, the English were unable to increase their area of control in Ireland. It was only in the sixteenth century that attempts were

again made to bring the whole of Ireland under English control.

It was King Henry VII (1485–1509) who began to restrict the power of the Irish aristocracy; and then his son, Henry VIII (1509–1547), had the Irish Parliament declare him King of Ireland. It was in the reign of Henry VIII that the seeds of the conflict in Ireland were sown.

Firstly, Henry changed the system of land ownership, by forcing the Irish lords to submit to his authority. The lords were given their land back if they did so.

Secondly, he caused much resentment with his anti-papal policies, after he split with the Pope in 1534. The Irish remained

Irish lords submitting
to the English
Governor of Ireland in
the 1570s

followers of the Catholic faith, and it was this that created insecurity in England in the sixteenth century. There was a fear that Ireland could be used as a base for invasion by England's Catholic enemies; and it was this fear that persuaded Queen Elizabeth I (1558–1603) to be ruthless in her treatment of those Irish lords who rebelled against her. The rebellions of the Earl of Desmond and the Earl of Tyrone were crushed, and Elizabeth could claim to have conquered most of Ireland.

The English plantation
of Ireland with
Protestant settlers

The Plantations

In order to increase England's security in Ireland, Elizabeth began a policy which was to have serious long-term consequences for the two countries. She gave loyal Protestant supporters land which had been confiscated from Catholic Irish rebels. This policy became known as PLANTATION, and it was adopted and extended greatly in the reign of King James I (1603–25). James was able to 'plant' his supporters following 'The flight of the earls', when 90 leading Ulster landowners fled after the Earl of Tyrone's rebellion was defeated in 1609. These supporters were a mixture of English and Scottish Protestants, and they were greatly resented by the Catholic population of Ulster.

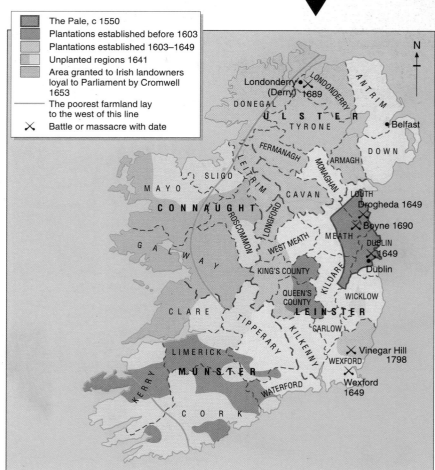

■	The Pale, c 1550
■	Plantations established before 1603
■	Plantations established 1603–1649
■	Unplanted regions 1641
■	Area granted to Irish landowners loyal to Parliament by Cromwell 1653
—	The poorest farmland lay to the west of this line
✕	Battle or massacre with date

In 1641, there was yet another rebellion against English rule, and about 12,000 Protestants died. For the Protestants, the rebellion served to increase their suspicion and hatred of the Catholics, and seemed to suggest that they would be a target for the Catholics in the future.

In 1641, the Roman Catholic Church decided to exterminate the Protestants in Ulster, and there took place one of the most bloody massacres in Irish history. It was led by the priests of the Roman Catholics and the rivers of Ulster ran red with Protestant blood. The River Bann was so choked with Protestant bodies that the Roman Catholics could walk dry-shod across the river.

Ian Paisley, September 1969.

Protestant settlers are murdered by Catholic rebels at Portadown in 1641

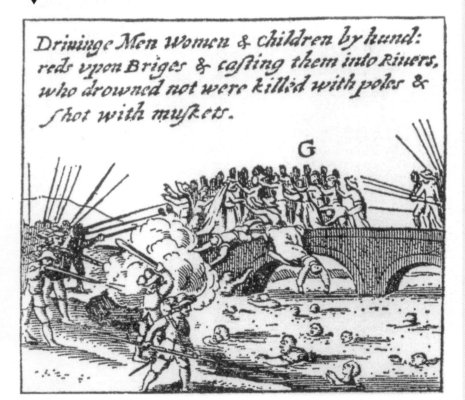

Drivinge Men Women & children by hund:
reds vpon Briges & casting them into Rivers,
who drowned not were killed with poles &
shot with muskets.

The rebellion was finally ended in 1649, when Oliver Cromwell crushed the Catholic rebels. In the two towns of Drogheda and Wexford, thousands of Catholics were killed. About eleven million acres of land were confiscated from Catholic landowners who had supported the rebels. Cromwell continued the policy of giving land to Protestant supporters and, by the time of his death in 1658, only a small part of all Irish land remained in the hands of Catholics.

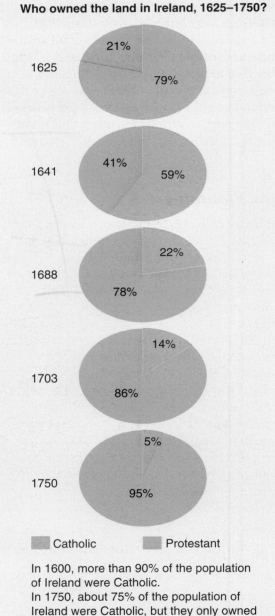

Who owned the land in Ireland, 1625–1750?

1625 — 21% / 79%

1641 — 41% / 59%

1688 — 22% / 78%

1703 — 14% / 86%

1750 — 5% / 95%

■ Catholic   ■ Protestant

In 1600, more than 90% of the population of Ireland were Catholic.
In 1750, about 75% of the population of Ireland were Catholic, but they only owned 5% of the land.

The Battle of the Boyne

However, there was no peace in Ireland after Cromwell's death. The troubles reached a climax in the years 1688–90, when King James II (1685–1688), who was a Catholic, was deposed as king for wanting to restore Roman Catholicism to England. James fled England and, in 1689, landed in Ireland. He hoped to use Ireland as a base to try to win back his throne, with the help of France. Meanwhile in England, a new king had been chosen – William of Orange, a Dutch Protestant. (William was James's son-in-law.) William of Orange took his army to Ireland and defeated James's army at the Battle of the Boyne, on 1 July 1690.

By 1700, Ulster had become mainly an Anglican and Presbyterian province, and the old Catholic ruling class had been displaced. Cut off from the Irish majority by their religion and culture, the 'New English' lived in a state of fear and hatred of the families whose land they had taken.

From *Great Britain an Irish Question* by P. Adelman, 1996.

So, by the arrival of William of Orange, the main ingredients of the conflict in Ireland already existed. There was the hatred of English rule, the dislike of the Protestant Church, and the issue of land ownership.

An artist's impression of James II fleeing to France after his defeat at the Battle of the Boyne in 1690

1. Explain in your own words how Ulster had become an 'Anglican province' by 1700.
2. Read Source B. Which part(s) of this source do you feel are the opinions or interpretations of the author? Explain your choice.
3. In what way does the picture of Portadown in 1641 seem to support Source B? Explain your answer.
4. Would an historian have any doubts about the reliability of Source B? Explain your answer fully.

2 The Unionists

After the success of William of Orange at the Battle of the Boyne, the Protestants in Ireland followed deliberate policies to ensure that the Catholics were treated as inferior citizens. The Irish Parliament was controlled by Protestants. They were determined to pass laws which would restrict the lives of the Catholic majority.

The Penal Laws (1697–1727), and the Protestant Ascendancy

The laws that were passed against Catholics were extremely severe. The main restrictions are listed below.

- No Catholic will be allowed to join the army or navy.
- Catholics who keep guns are liable to be whipped.
- No Catholic, when he dies, may pass on his land as a whole to one son. He must divide it between all his sons. However, if one of his sons becomes a Protestant, then he will inherit the whole of the land.
- A Catholic may only buy land or lease it for 31 years.
- No Catholic will be allowed to vote, or become a Member of Parliament, or a town councillor. No Catholic may join the civil service. No Catholic may become a solicitor or a lawyer.
- Catholics may not receive higher education or take professional jobs.

These Penal Laws paved the way for what became known as 'the Protestant Ascendancy' in Ireland – that is the control of Ireland by an elite group of Anglican Protestants. The Anglican Church of Ireland had great power, wealth, influence, and many privileges, even though it represented only 1 in 7 of the people of Ireland. Many of the Protestant landowners preferred not to live in Ireland – they were the 'absentee landlords' who made money from the rents which their tenants paid. The Catholics had the poorest farmland in the west of Ireland and were generally very poor. Even when Catholics were allowed to buy and hold leases on land, after 1782, there were outbreaks of violence. Protestant gangs (The Peep O'Day Boys) fought Catholic gangs (The Defenders). After continued violence, and the Battle of the Diamond in 1795, the Protestants formed the Orange Order to protect the interests of the Protestant community.

I do solemnly and sincerely swear of my own free will and accord that I will to the utmost of my power support and defend the present King George III and all the heirs of the Crown, so long as they support the Protestant Ascendancy, the constitution and the laws of these kingdoms; and I do further swear that I am not, nor ever was, a Roman Catholic or papist; that I was not nor ever will be, a United Irishman, and that I never took an oath of secrecy to that Society.

The oath of the Orange Order, 1795.

Bitterness between the two communities did not diminish and, after the defeat of the United Irishmen in 1798 (see page 13), the Government in London decided that Ireland should no longer have its own Parliament. The *Act of Union* of 1800 abolished the status of Ireland as a separate kingdom, and in future Irish MPs would have to sit at Westminster.

The kingdom of Great Britain and Ireland shall, on 1 January 1801... and for ever, be united into one kingdom by the name 'The United Kingdom of Great Britain and Ireland'. The United Kingdom shall be represented in one and the same Parliament. 32 Irish bishops and lords will sit in the House of Lords and 100 commoners will sit and vote on the part of Ireland in the House of Commons.

An extract from the *Act of Union*, 1800.

Home Rule

There was much opposition to the *Act of Union* in Ireland in the nineteenth century (see page 17). Politicians in England gradually came to realise that reforms were necessary if the Union was going to be maintained without alienating the whole of the Catholic population of Ireland. Therefore, some reforms were made throughout the century, leading to the introduction of the First Home Rule Bill in 1886 by Prime Minister William Gladstone.

However, this Bill now alienated the Protestants of Ulster. The Protestant majority in Ulster felt that Home Rule, and a separate Parliament, would lead eventually to an independent Ireland. This would then lead to Catholic supremacy over the Irish Protestants. The Protestant reaction to the proposed introduction of

Home Rule was a revival of the Orange Order and the formation of the Ulster Loyalist Anti-Repeal Union.

There should be reasonable safeguards for the Protestant minority, especially in the province of Ulster.
But I cannot allow it to be said that a Protestant minority, in Ulster or elsewhere, is to rule the question at large for Ireland, when five-sixths of its chosen representatives are of one mind on the matter.

From William Gladstone's speech in the House of Commons, 1886.

Prime Minister William Gladstone leading a debate in the House of Commons on the Home Rule Bill

The introduction of the Home Rule Bill had a significant impact on politics in Britain. Several Ulster Liberal MPs broke away from the Liberal Party and joined the Conservatives, who were completely opposed to granting Home Rule. Politics in Ulster also changed in the 1880s, and was focussed purely around the issue of Home Rule. The formation of an Ulster Defence Association in 1886, and the visit of Lord Randolph Churchill, seemed to predict a violent future.

Home Rule is Rome Rule

A common saying in Ulster in the 1880s.

If political parties and political leaders should be so utterly lost to every feeling of courage and honour as to hand over, for the sake of buying a short period of parliamentary tranquillity, the lives and liberties of the loyalists of Ireland to their hereditary and most bitter foes, make no doubt on this point – Ulster will not be a consenting party... Ulster will fight and Ulster will be right.

Lord Randolph Churchill's open letter to a Liberal Unionist, 1886.

There was, in fact, an outbreak of sectarian violence in Ulster in 1886, when 32 people were killed, scores were injured, and the police sustained some 340 injuries. The First and Second Home Rule Bills of 1886 and 1893 failed. The Conservatives and the Liberal Unionists would never give their approval to such Bills.

When the Conservatives were in power between 1893 and 1905, they tried to introduce changes which would remove the demand for Home Rule. Their policy was known as 'Killing Home Rule with kindness', but it served only to antagonise the Ulster Unionists further, because they felt that the changes favoured the Catholics. In 1905, the Ulster Unionist Council was formed in order to protect the interests of the Protestant community. The Council represented every branch of Unionism – the Orange Order, Unionist Clubs, Ulster MPs, the Protestant Church, and Ulster lords.

It seemed as if neither the Liberals nor the Conservatives were able to develop policies in Ireland which were capable of keeping the two communities satisfied. The issue of Home Rule re-emerged after 1910. However, it did so not because of events in Ireland, but because of events in Great Britain. There were two general elections in 1910, and, after the second, the Liberals no longer had a majority in the Commons. In order to remain in office, the Liberals had to rely on the support of the Irish Nationalist MPs. The price of the Nationalists' support was the introduction of a Third Home Rule Bill. The Bill was introduced in 1912 and, because of the recent constitutional crisis and changes to the powers of the House of Lords, the Bill would almost certainly become law in 1914.

An Irish Parliament would be set up with a nominated Senate and an elected House of Commons.
42 Irish MPs would still represent Ireland at Westminster.

Main points of the 1912 Third Home Rule Bill.

The main point about the Bill was that Ulster was to be included in the new self-governing Ireland. This created a tremendous stir in Unionist circles, and the gulf between them and the Liberal Government became ever wider. Edward Carson and James Craig, the leaders of the Ulster Unionists, began to speak in terms of armed resistance to the Bill, and thus the Government. Huge meetings were organised and there were military-style demonstrations. On Easter Tuesday 1912, over 100,000 marched against the introduction of the Bill into the House of Commons. This was followed by the signing of the Solemn League and Covenant on 28 September 1912. More than 500,000 men and women signed. It was reported that some men signed in their own blood.

 The Ulster Unionist leader, Sir Edward Carson, signing the Covenant against the Third Home Rule Bill in September 1912

A *Punch* cartoon showing the Nationalist leader, John Redmond, trying to herd all of Ireland through the Home Rule gate. The Protestant counties of Ulster are trying to get away.

Being convinced in our consciences that Home Rule would be disastrous to the material well-being of Ulster, as well as of the whole of Ireland, subversive of our civil and religious freedom, destructive of our citizenship, and perilous to the unity of the Empire, we, whose names are underwritten, men of Ulster, loyal subjects of his Glorious Majesty King George V, humbly relying on the God whom our fathers... confidently trusted, do hereby pledge ourselves in solemn covenant throughout this our time of threatened calamity to stand by one another in defending our cherished position of equal citizenship in the United Kingdom, and in using all means which may be found necessary to defeat the present conspiracy to set up a Home Rule Parliament in Ireland. And in the event of such a Parliament being forced upon us, we further and mutually pledge ourselves to refuse to recognise its authority. In sure confidence that God will defend the right.

The Solemn League and Covenant, 1912.

SECOND THOUGHTS.

The Unionists were angered by the Third Home Rule Bill because there were no safeguards for minority groups. In order to protect themselves – as a minority – the Ulster Volunteer Force was born. The force

BRAVO, ULSTER! UNLOADING THE GUNS AT DONAGHADEE.

Historic Events Series

No. 6

A postcard of the time commemorating the arming of the Ulster Unionists in 1914

quickly recruited men and trained and drilled them as soldiers. The organisation soon had more than 100,000 members. More importantly, the UVF had access to huge funds of £1,000,000, and this money was used to buy weapons. For example, in April 1914, 35,000 rifles and 5,000,000 rounds of ammunition were bought from Germany and landed at Larne.

The Ulster Unionists were now in a position to fight against the British Government. The situation was not improved when the Irish Volunteers (see page 19) also received weapons, It seemed as if Ireland was on the verge of civil war. However, events in Europe overtook both sides when Britain declared war on Germany on 4 August 1914. Prime Minister Asquith decided to place the *Home Rule Act* on the statute books, but to suspend its provisions until the end of the war with Germany. The men of Ulster joined the British army in huge numbers, just as many of their fellow Irishmen in the South did. By 1916, about 150,000 had volunteered, but even here the British Government managed to irritate the South. A special Ulster Division was formed; and on the political front, Edward Carson, the leader of the Ulster Unionist MPs, became a member of Asquith's wartime government.

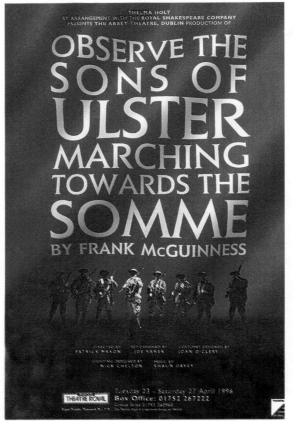

A poster advertising a modern play about the Ulster Division at the Battle of the Somme, 1916

1   Using this chapter, write an explanation of each of the following terms:
    Act of Union; Home Rule; Orange Order; Unionist.

2   Why were the Unionists so opposed to Home Rule?

3 The Republicans

As you have seen in Chapter 2, the Protestants were able to secure control of Ireland by means of the Penal Laws. However, opposition to the power of the Anglican Protestants grew; and the influence of the American and French Revolutions helped to spark rebellion in Ireland at the end of the 1790s. The Society of United Irishmen was intent on ending English rule and sought to win the support of all Irishmen.

United Irishmen to Young Irelanders

We think it our duty as Irishmen to state what we feel to be our heavy grievance. We have no national government, we are ruled by Englishmen and the servants of Englishmen, whose object of interest is another country. This Society is constituted for the purpose of forwarding a union of power among Irishmen of every religious persuasion.

An extract from the constitution of the United Irishmen, 1797.

The first rebellion was in 1798, led by Wolfe Tone (see biography on page 14). Tone was a Protestant who wanted Ireland to be independent of all control from Britain. Tone won the support of many Catholics and Presbyterians (Protestants who were not members of the Church of Ireland). The rebellion failed and Tone's forces were defeated at the Battle of Vinegar Hill. More than 50,000 people were killed – many in cold blood. (A further rebellion in 1803, led by Robert Emmett, also failed.)

British troops defeat the Irish rebel forces at the battle of Vinegar Hill in June 1798

Theobald Wolfe Tone

A painting of Wolfe Tone in uniform

▼ Born 1764
▼ Protestant lawyer and leader of the United Irishmen
▼ Active in the 1798 rebellion
▼ Captured on board a ship bound for France and committed suicide in prison

Wolfe Tone is regarded as a hero by modern day Republicans. His grave in Bodenstown churchyard has been the site of many Republican gatherings, and important speeches have been made there

My aim was to break the connection with England and win independence. To do this we had to forget past differences and replace the words 'Protestant' and 'Catholic' with the one name of 'Irishman'.

From Wolfe Tone's autobiography.

Six hundred years of slavery have passed over our fathers' heads. It is England who deprives our wretched peasantry of their rights as human beings. You must choose between slavery or independence. I do not doubt your decision: liberty for yourselves and independence for your country.

Wolfe Tone's address to the people of Ireland.

We have come here not just to salute this noble dust and pay our homage to the noble spirit of Wolfe Tone. We have come to express once more that we accept the gospel of Irish Nationalism which he was the first to express in worthy terms. His voice rings out through Ireland calling to us from this grave, 'break the connection with England, the source of all our political evils.'

Patrick Pearse, speaking at Wolfe Tone's grave in 1913.

There is then, an irony in the Irish conflict. A major rebellion against the English was led by a Protestant; and this rebellion convinced the English Government to introduce the *Act of Union* (see page 9). However, the *Act of Union* did not bring about a settled Ireland. Daniel O'Connell formed the Catholic Association in 1823 to help tenants and to fight for the right of Catholics to become MPs at Westminster. O'Connell won tremendous support in Ireland and forced the removal of restrictions on Catholics. The *Catholic Emancipation Act* of 1829 allowed Irish Catholics to become MPs.

O'Connell wanted to go even further, and he set up The Repeal Association through which he campaigned for the ending of the *Act of Union*. When O'Connell died in 1847, the Association faded away. However, some members of the Association had become prominent in the 1840s in the Young Ireland Movement. The Young Irelanders organised a rebellion in 1848, but this failed and the leaders were transported to Tasmania.

You English are unable to govern Ireland even to your own satisfaction; for two-thirds of the time you have ruled her, not by the powers of the law, but by undisguised despotism, and her misery has been of no advantage to you. In the name of Ireland, I call upon you to do my country justice. I call upon you to restore her national independence.

An extract from a speech by Daniel O'Connell, date unknown.

The Irish people should fight to set up a republic completely cut off from Britain... Speeches and resolutions never will do one bit of good unless we all have arms and are ready to turn out.

An extract from the newspaper *The United Irishman*, 1847.

The Great Famine

In fact, it was an agricultural disaster in the 1840s which led to a long-lasting hatred of the English. In 1845 and 1846, the potato crop failed. The Irish farmers and their families depended on this crop as a major part of their diet – the crop failure resulted in at least one million deaths. In order to escape famine, about one and a half million people emigrated, many going to the USA.

The suffering of the Famine and the depopulation of the country did more than anything else to embitter Irish attitudes towards England. And the memory was kept alive, not just in Ireland, but in the communities of Irish people who resettled in Britain, North America, and elsewhere.

From a British History textbook written in 1977.

A people whose land and lives are in the keeping and custody of others, instead of their own, are not in a position of common safety. The Irish Famine of 1846 is example and proof. The corn crops were sufficient to feed the island. But the landlords would have their rents in spite of the famine... They took the whole harvest and left hunger to those who raised it. Had the people of Ireland been the landlords of Ireland, not a single human creature would have died of hunger.

James Fintan Lalor, a Young Irelander writing in June 1848.

Police and soldiers evict a Catholic Irish family from their home in the 1880s. Evictions like this were a common sight throughout the nineteenth century. Many of the evicted ended up emigrating to countries like America, from where their descendants have given support to the IRA (see pages 61–63).

The Republican revival

Republican pressure on the British continued in the 1850s with the formation of the Irish Republican Brotherhood. (The IRB were also known as the Fenians, in honour of the forces of Finn MacCool, the legendary Irish hero.) The IRB were committed to the overthrow of British power and sought to set up an independent Irish republic. The movement was founded by James Stephens, an ex-Young Irelander. Stephens and the IRB gained a huge amount of publicity in the 1860s by means of terrorist activities, such as those below in 1867.

- An armed rebellion failed.
- Three Irishmen were captured and hanged in Manchester after releasing two Fenian prisoners. They became known as the Manchester Martyrs.
- In December there was an attempt to rescue a Fenian imprisoned in Clerkenwell Prison, London. Part of the prison wall was blown up and twelve people were killed and fifty injured.

A picture printed and published in America in support of the Manchester Martyrs

IRELANDS LATEST MARTYRS.

The Fenian movement declined after these events. Yet, they did seem to have some impact on the Government at Westminster. William Gladstone, the Prime Minister, brought in reforms which he hoped would tackle the causes of unrest in Ireland. The Church of Ireland was disestablished. This now meant that all religious denominations were placed on an equal footing. By the 1870 *Land Act*, and subsequent ones, Gladstone hoped to protect tenants who were unjustly evicted. However, the reforms did little to solve the key issue – that many Irish people resented the *Act of Union* and did not wish to be ruled from Westminster. The call for change seemed to be answered in 1873, when the Home Rule League was formed.

We declare our conviction that it is necessary to the peace and prosperity of Ireland that the right of domestic legislation on all Irish affairs should be restored to our country. We claim the privilege of managing our own affairs by a parliament assembled in Ireland. There should be in Ireland a government for Irish affairs, controlled by the Irish Parliament.

Extracts from the aims of the Home Rule League, 1873.

During the next twelve years, the Home Rule League had great successes in the general elections – see below.

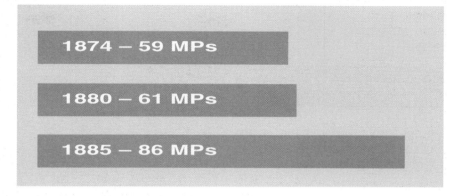

These 'Nationalist' MPs were a distinct, cohesive group who were pushing for a form of separation from England in a democratic manner. However, their success frightened the Liberal MPs in Ulster, who felt that Home Rule would inevitably lead to complete independence for Ireland. The 'Irish Nationalist' MPs supported the two Home Rule Bills which Gladstone introduced (1886 and 1893), but found themselves outmanoeuvred by the Conservatives and the Liberal Unionists. After the failure of the Second Bill, Irish Nationalism seemed to stall. Their great leader, Charles Parnell, had been disgraced and the Party split. A revival came in 1905 when a new Party emerged – Sinn Fein (We Ourselves) – formed by Arthur Griffith. There was also a revival of the IRB, which announced that it would seek to gain independence by an armed revolution.

1   Using this chapter, write an explanation of each of the following terms:
    Fenian; Home Rule League; Irish Republican Brotherhood; Republican; United Irishmen.

Charles Stewart Parnell

Parnell is removed from the British House of Commons for obstructing Parliament

- ▼ Born in Avondale in 1846
- ▼ Educated in England at Cambridge University
- ▼ Became an MP in 1875
- ▼ Elected President of the National Land League in 1879
- ▼ Imprisoned in 1881 after inciting law breaking
- ▼ Leader of the Home Rule League in Parliament.
- ▼ Named in a divorce suit in 1889 by his colleague William O'Shea
- ▼ Died in England in 1891

Parnell entered politics at the age of 29, and soon became involved with the Irish land issue. He joined and became President of the National Land League, which later became the Irish National League. He supported Gladstone and the Liberals in the 1880 elections, but joined the opposition when he saw that Gladstone's reforms did not go far enough. Through the Land League he recommended the breaking of the new Land Laws, and was put in jail in 1881. In 1885, Parnell used his political power to bring down the Liberal government, when his Irish MPs voted against the extension of antiterrorist laws.

His influence amongst the Irish declined after 1889, when he was named in a divorce case. He had been having an affair with the wife of one of his colleagues. The resulting scandal split the Home Rule League. Parnell died in Brighton, England in 1891.

When Home Rule became a certainty after the passing of the Third Bill in 1912, and Ulster began arming (see page 12), the IRB could see that a civil war was a possibility in Ireland.

The effect of the arming of Ulster on the rest of Ireland was not immediate, but the IRB realised that Carson and the Ulster Unionists had opened a door that could not easily be closed again. By way of getting ready, the Dublin Officers of the IRB ordered the members in the city to be taught military drill... at the same time the IRB began to buy a few rifles, but the funds available for such purposes were very small.

From *The Irish Volunteers*, written in 1963.

The IRB armed themselves and set up the Irish Volunteers, and, by May 1914, had about 80,000 members. A second force also emerged at this time, the Irish Citizen Army. This group developed as a result of the violence used by police on the transport strikers in Dublin that year. However, when war against Germany was declared in August 1914, many men of the South volunteered for the British army, just as their counterparts did in Ulster. Ominously, though, there were some Nationalists who felt that England's war against Germany might be used to their advantage.

We have no foreign enemy except the treacherous government of England – a government even whilst it is calling us to die for it, refuses to give a straight answer to our demand for Home Rule.

James Connolly, Irish Citizen Army leader, 1914.

Full steam ahead, John Redmond* said,
That everything was well, chum;
Home Rule will come when we are dead
And buried out in Belgium.

A rhyme published in James Connolly's paper *Workers' Republic* in 1915. *Redmond was leader of the Irish Nationalist MPs.

A British recruitment poster used in Ireland during the First World War

4. *F*rom Easter Rising to Civil War, 1916–1923

The war against Germany deflected much of the tension about Home Rule. However, there were many Irish Volunteers who refused to fight in the war, and they decided to plan a rising against the British.

Three weeks after the war had started, a meeting was held at which it was decided that Ireland should make use of the opportunity of the European war to rise in rebellion against England. There were eight or nine people at that meeting, including Patrick Pearse, Arthur Griffith, Tom Clarke, Sean MacDermott, and Eamonn Ceannt.

Sean Kelly, an Irish Volunteer, writing in 1915.

The Irish Volunteers and the Irish Citizen Army planned to seize control of Dublin at Easter 1916. However, things did not go according to plan. The British navy captured a German ship which was carrying 20,000 rifles and ammunition for the Volunteers; and Sir Roger Casement, a leading Irish Nationalist, was also captured. Despite these setbacks, the decision was taken by Patrick Pearse and James Connolly, the leaders of the two groups, to go ahead with the Rising.

The Rising began on Easter Monday (24 April 1916), and the rebels made their headquarters in the Post Office building. Pearse proclaimed that Ireland was an independent republic and the Irish tricolour flag was raised.

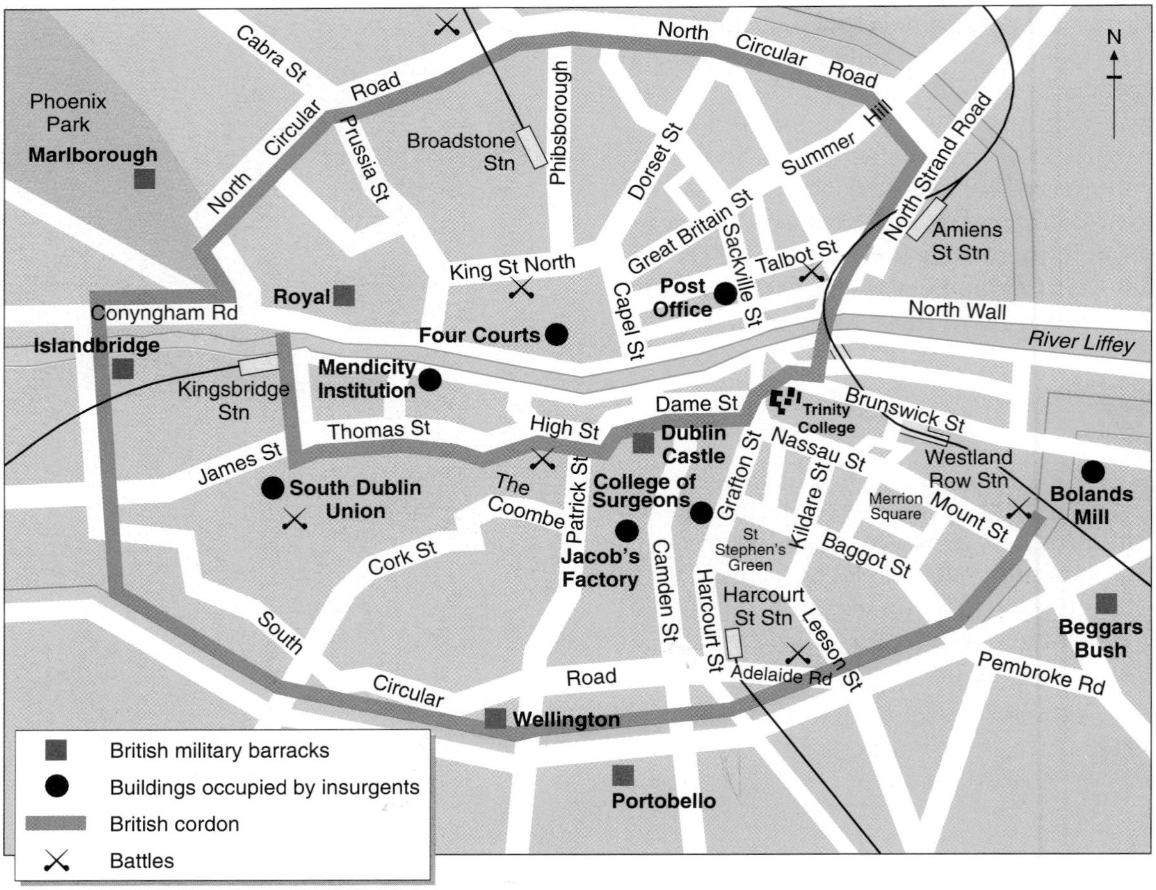

► A map of the centre of Dublin during the Easter Rising

Map labels: Cabra St, North Circular Road, North Circular Road, Phibsborough, Summer Hill, North Strand Road, N, Phoenix Park, Marlborough, Prussia St, Broadstone Stn, Dorset St, Great Britain St, Sackville St, Talbot St, Amiens St Stn, King St North, Capel St, Post Office, North Wall, Royal, Conyngham Rd, River Liffey, Islandbridge, Four Courts, Kingsbridge Stn, Mendicity Institution, Dame St, Trinity College, Brunswick St, Thomas St, High St, Dublin Castle, Grafton St, Nassau St, Westland Row Stn, James St, The Coombe, Patrick St, College of Surgeons, Kildare St, Merrion Square, Mount St, Bolands Mill, South Dublin Union, Jacob's Factory, Camden St, St Stephen's Green, Baggot St, Cork St, Harcourt St, Harcourt St Stn, Leeson St, Beggars Bush, South, Adelaide Rd, Pembroke Rd, Circular, Road, Wellington, Portobello

Legend:
- British military barracks
- ● Buildings occupied by insurgents
- British cordon
- ✕ Battles

There were about 2,000 rebels (estimates vary of the numbers involved) and they were quickly defeated by the British, who used not only artillery but a gunboat stationed on the River Liffey. The table right gives some statistics about the Rising.

Civilians killed	220
Rebels killed	64
British soldiers and police killed	134
British soldiers wounded	381
Arrested	3000
Interned	1867
Damage to buildings etc	£2.5 million

 The ruined centre of Dublin after the defeat of the Easter Rising

The majority of the Irish population were shocked by the Easter Rising. After their arrest, the rebels were marched away by the British soldiers and were verbally abused by the civilian population.

B

A raucous crowd came pouring out of the houses and the side streets to accost the rebels. Waving British flags, they shouted 'Murderers! Guttersnipes!' The flood of insults was fierce. These were the people for whose freedom the rebels had just been risking death.

An eye-witness account quoted in *Agony at Easter*, written in 1969.

THE SINN FEIN RISING AS IT AFFECTED PEOPLE

 A page from the English newspaper *The Graphic*, with a special feature on the Easter Rising and the suffering it caused in Dublin. It was published on 13 May 1916.

THE PROCLAMATION OF
POBLACHT NA H EIREANN.
THE PROVISIONAL GOVERNMENT
OF THE
IRISH REPUBLIC
TO THE PEOPLE OF IRELAND.

IRISHMEN AND IRISHWOMEN: In the name of God and of the dead generations from which she receives her old tradition of nationhood, Ireland, through us, summons her children to her flag and strikes for her freedom.

Having organised and trained her manhood through her secret revolutionary organisation, the Irish Republican Brotherhood, and through her open military organisations, the Irish Volunteers and the Irish Citizen Army, having patiently perfected her discipline, having resolutely waited for the right moment to reveal itself, she now seizes that moment, and, supported by her exiled children in America and by gallant allies in Europe, but relying in the first on her own strength, she strikes in full confidence of victory.

We declare the right of the people of Ireland to the ownership of Ireland, and to the unfettered control of Irish destinies, to be sovereign and indefeasible. The long usurpation of that right by a foreign people and government has not extinguished the right, nor can it ever be extinguished except by the destruction of the Irish people. In every generation the Irish people have asserted their right to national freedom and sovereignty; six times during the past three hundred years they have asserted it in arms. Standing on that fundamental right and again asserting it in arms in the face of the world, we hereby proclaim the Irish Republic as a Sovereign Independent State, and we pledge our lives and the lives of our comrades-in-arms to the cause of its freedom of its welfare, and of its exaltation among the nations.

The Irish Republic is entitled to, and hereby claims, the allegiance of every Irishman and Irishwoman. The Republic guarantees religious and civil liberty, equal rights and equal opportunities to all its citizens, and declares its resolve to pursue the happiness and prosperity of the whole nation and of all its parts, cherishing all the children of the nation equally, and oblivious of the differences carefully fostered by an alien government, which have divided a minority from the majority in the past.

Until our arms have brought the opportune moment for the establishment of a permanent National Government, representative of the whole people of Ireland and elected by the suffrages of all her men and women, the Provisional Government, hereby constituted, will administer the civil and military affairs of the Republic in trust for the people.

We place the cause of the Irish Republic under the protection of the Most High God, Whose blessing we invoke upon our arms, and we pray that no one who serves that cause will dishonour it by cowardice, inhumanity, or rapine. In this supreme hour the Irish nation must, by its valour and discipline and by the readiness of its children to sacrifice themselves for the common good, prove itself worthy of the august destiny to which it is called.

Signed on Behalf of the Provisional Government,
THOMAS J. CLARKE.
SEAN Mac DIARMADA, THOMAS MacDONAGH,
P. H. PEARSE, EAMONN CEANNT,
JAMES CONNOLLY. JOSEPH PLUNKETT

A

This is the Irish Proclamation of Independence, read by Patrick Pearse on the steps of the Post Office building in Dublin in 1916. Pearse was leader of the Irish Volunteers. You can see that Pearse has signed it, and so has James Connolly (leader of the Irish Citizen Army). When the rebels surrendered a few days later, both Connolly's and Pearse's signatures were needed to stop the rebels fighting.

Connolly was a trade unionist and Socialist who wanted to bring about Irish Independence as part of his aim to establish a Socialist state. He formed the Irish Citizen Army in 1913, which then joined forces with the Irish Volunteers in 1916. The flag of the Citizen Army was the 'Plough and Stars'. It afterwards featured as the title of a play about the Easter Rising written by Sean O'Casey (see page 32).

Pearse led the IRB and its army, the Irish Volunteers. In April 1916, Pearse declared himself the Commandant-General of a joint Irish republican army. Pearse seemed to have believed that it was necessary for Ireland to have its martyrs.

B

Life springs from death; and from the graves of patriot men and women spring living nations. The Defenders of this Realm think they have pacified Ireland, but the fools, the fools, the fools! They have left us our Fenian dead, and while Ireland holds these graves, Ireland unfree shall never be at peace.

Patrick Pearse speaking at the funeral of the Fenian O'Donovan Rossa in 1915.

 Some of James Connolly's Irish Citizen Army parade outside Liberty Hall, Dublin, the head office of the Irish Transport Workers Union. When he was asked if there was any chance of success at all, he replied: 'None whatsoever, we are going out to be slaughtered.'

First voice: 'We thought it a foolish thing for four score [80] to go into battle against four thousand, or maybe forty thousand.'

Second voice: 'And so it is a foolish thing. Do you want us to be wise?'

Lines from a play called *The Singer*, written by Pearse in 1915.

Connolly and Pearse were later shot by the British for their part in the Rising.

1 Using Source A and the text in this feature, can you work out the links between the IRB, the Irish Volunteers and the Irish Citizen Army?

2 How reliable is Source C as evidence of the strength of the Irish Citizen Army in 1916? Explain your answer.

3 What evidence can you find in Sources B, C and D that Connolly and Pearse knew the Easter Rising would fail?

4 In the light of your answer to Question 3, how valid were the proclamations and claims made in Source A? Explain your answer.

5 Using this feature, and information from the rest of this chapter, how important were James Connolly and Patrick Pearse in the Easter Rising?

A

Rebel casualties – 64 killed, an unknown number wounded
British casualties – 134 killed, 381 wounded
Civilian casualties – 220 killed, 600 wounded

The human cost of the Easter Rising.

B

3 May 1916, Patrick Pearse, MacDonagh, and Clarke were shot at dawn in Kilmainham Jail, Dublin
4 May 1916, Plunket, Daly, O'Hannrahan, and William Pearse were shot in Dublin
5 May 1916, MacBride was shot in Dublin
8 May 1916, Colbert, Ceannt, Mallin, and Heuston were shot in Dublin
9 May 1916 Thomas Kent was shot in Cork
12 May 1916, Connolly, strapped seated to a chair because of leg wounds, and MacDermott were shot in Dublin
3 August 1916, Roger Casement was hanged in Pentonville Prison, London

The fate of some of the rebels who took part in the Rising.

The execution of one of the rebel leaders in May 1916

C

Dublin – Connolly, Heuston, Pearse
London – Kings Cross, Victoria, Waterloo

Mainline railway stations in Dublin and London.

D

Oh but we talked at large before
The sixteen men were shot,
But who can talk of give and take, What should be and should not
While those dead men are loitering there
To stir the boiling pot?

A poem about the executions by W B Yeats.

E

In 1916 I was in the Middle East with the British army. I saw a notice about the rising in Dublin and about the executions. I said to myself, 'What the hell am I doing with the British army? It's with the Irish I should be.'

Adapted from Tom Barry's *Curious Journey*, 1982. Barry later joined the IRA and became one of its leaders.

1 How does Source A help explain why thousands of people in Dublin were bitterly opposed to the rebellion?
2 Look at Source B. Why do you think the executions were strung out over so many days? What effect might this have had on the Irish people?
3 What are the London railway stations named after? What are the Dublin railway stations named after?
4 What does this tell you about the impact of the Easter Rising and the executions on the Irish?
5 Read Source D. What do you think Yeats meant by the line, 'To stir the boiling pot'?
6 According to Sources D and E, how did the executions start to affect Irish opinion?
7 Using the sources in this feature, and information from the rest of this chapter, explain why the Easter Rising was a turning point in the Irish struggle for independence.

The British lost the support of many Irish people by executing the rebel leaders.

> The great bulk of the population were not favourable to the rebels... they got no popular support whatsoever. What is happening is that thousands of people in Dublin, who ten days ago were bitterly opposed to the whole of the Sinn Fein movement, and to the rebellion, are now becoming infuriated against the Government on account of these executions, and, as I am informed... that feeling is spreading throughout the country in a most dangerous degree.

John Dillon speaking in the House of Commons on 11 May, 1916. Dillon was a leading Nationalist MP.

> We seem to have lost. We have not lost. To refuse to fight would have been to lose. To fight is to win. We have kept faith with the past and handed a tradition to the future. If our deed has not been sufficient to win freedom, then our children will win it by a better deed.

Patrick Pearse speaking at his court-martial, 2 May 1916.

The British Government compounded its errors by imposing martial law on Ireland and imprisoning people such as Arthur Griffith. As a result, the popularity of Sinn Fein increased and, by the end of 1916, Sinn Fein had developed into a revolutionary party committed to the creation of an independent united Ireland. Sinn Fein's popularity was made clear in 1917, when it won two parliamentary by-elections in what had been safe Nationalist seats. In that year, Eamon de Valera (see pages 36–38) won the East Clare seat for

the Party. At the end of 1917, there were about 250,000 members of Sinn Fein. It was emerging as a Party powerful enough to challenge the Irish Nationalists.

However, the British Government did continue trying to solve the conflict, and, in 1917, set up the Convention. This body lasted from July 1917 to April 1918, but it was doomed to failure when Sinn Fein boycotted it. Equally important for the British was the continued opposition of the Ulster Unionists.

Further British incompetence occurred in May 1918, when the Government tried to introduce conscription into Ireland. John Dillon, the new leader of the Nationalists, told Lloyd George that the policy was utter madness: 'All Ireland will rise against you.' Dillon was proved right. The Irish Nationalists walked out of Westminster and, together with Sinn Fein, organised an anti-conscription campaign. Trade Unions in Ireland organised a general strike, and the Roman Catholic Church openly denounced conscription as an inhumane policy. A National Pledge was drawn up and it was as a result of this united opposition that Lloyd George decided not to introduce conscription into Ireland. It was becoming clear that Sinn Fein was adopting the role of the leading opponents of British rule in Ireland. In the general election of 1918, the political face of Ireland changed for ever. Sinn Fein won 73 seats and the Irish Nationalists won only 7. The Manifesto of Sinn Fein had been unambiguous about its aims (see next page).

A Sinn Fein election poster from the 1918 election

Sinn Fein aims at securing the establishment of the Irish Republic by:

a withdrawing the Irish MPs from Westminster... and opposing the will of the British Government or any other foreign government to make laws for Ireland.

b making use of any means available to render useless the power of England to hold Ireland in subjection by military force.

c establishing a Parliament as the supreme national authority to speak and act in the name of the Irish people.

d appealing to the Peace Conference [this drew up the peace treaties after the end of the First World War in 1918] for the establishment of Ireland as an independent nation.

Sinn Fein also stands by the Proclamation of the Provisional Government of Easter 1916.

Sinn Fein Manifesto 1918.

Countess Markievicz

Countess Markievicz photographed in 1919, shortly after being released from prison in Cork

▼ Born into a Protestant landowning family in County Sligo
▼ Married a Polish Count
▼ Led a group of Republican rebels in the 1916 Easter Rising
▼ First woman to be elected to the British Parliament, 1918
▼ Minister of Labour in the Irish Dail, 1919

Constance Gore Booth, the Countess Markievicz, seems the most unlikely Republican leader – a Protestant and a wealthy landowner. She was educated in London and Paris, and married a Polish Count. She enjoyed writing and painting, and was keen on fox-hunting. In 1904, she attended fashionable parties in Dublin Castle. Then, in 1908, she became a Republican, joining the 'Daughters of Ireland'. A year later she was elected to the council of Sinn Fein. In the Easter Rising (1916) she commanded a group of Volunteers who captured the Royal College of Surgeons Building in Dublin. When she came out of the building, in full Irish Republican Brotherhood (IRB) uniform, the British officer who took her surrender could not believe she had been in charge.

Markievicz was imprisoned for her part in the Rising, but later was released and elected to the British Parliament in 1918. Constance Markievicz was the first woman to be elected to the British House of Commons, though as a Sinn Fein MP she refused to take her seat.

True to their promise, the Sinn Fein MPs did not take up their seats, though the 23 Ulster MPs did. The split was made more clear when the Sinn Fein Party set up the Dail Eireann in Dublin (Parliament of Ireland). There they made the Irish Declaration of Independence on 21 January 1919.

English rule in this country is and has always been based on force...

We confirm the establishment of the Irish Republic and pledge ourselves and our people to make this declaration effective by every means at our command.

We solemnly declare foreign government in Ireland to be an invasion of our national right which we will never tolerate, and we demand the evacuation of our country by the English garrison.

Extract from the Declaration of Independence, January 1919.

When the Dail first met, only 25 of the Sinn Fein MPs were present – 34 were in prison and Michael Collins (see page 30) was absent because he was masterminding the escape of Eamon de Valera from prison in England. Later in the year, de Valera was made President, Arthur Griffith Vice-President and Michael Collins the Minister of Finance. The 'illegal' government even began to collect taxes.

In January 1919, the Irish Republican Army (the new name for the Irish Citizen Army and the Irish Volunteers) carried out an attack on two policemen of the Royal Irish Constabulary. The constables were killed. For the IRA and its military leader, Michael Collins, this was the opening phase of what was regarded by the Republicans as the 'War of Independence'. Guerrilla attacks continued throughout 1919 and, in September, the British Government banned the Dail and also Sinn Fein. Nevertheless, the IRA continued its attacks on the RIC and the British army – as far as they were concerned, they were at war with Britain.

Dail Eireann declares that a state of war exists between Ireland and England. Every Volunteer is entitled to use all legitimate methods of warfare against the soldiers and policemen of the English usurper, and to slay them if it is necessary to do so in order to overcome their resistance.

An extract from the *Volunteer's Journal*, 1919.

Lloyd George and the British Government did not have a positive policy to combat the IRA and Sinn Fein, apart from repression, and this antagonised the ordinary civilian population. It was also difficult to maintain law and order – the IRA killed 176 policemen in 1920, and 54 soldiers, and the situation was made worse because hundreds of RIC constables were resigning in fear of their lives. The RIC had to be strengthened by the recruitment of about 7,000 ex-soldiers, who were given the nickname 'Black and Tans' (they wore khaki uniforms with the black belts and peaked caps of the RIC). Another security force had to be created in 1920 in order to replace those officers who were resigning from the RIC. This new force, the Auxiliaries, was composed of ex-army officers, who turned out to be an ill-disciplined and violent group.

The IRA widened the scope of its attacks in 1920 – civilians and public buildings were targeted and there were many atrocities. The Black and Tans and Auxiliaries followed these attacks with their own atrocities, which served only to push the Irish civilians towards Sinn Fein and the IRA. Perhaps the worst incidents of the war took place on 21 November 1920, on what became known as 'Bloody Sunday' (see page 50). The IRA killed 12 British agents and 2 Auxiliaries, the Black and Tans retaliated by firing into a Gaelic football match, killing 12 and injuring 60. A week later, the IRA attacked a convoy of Auxiliaries and killed 18. The retaliation this time was an attack by the Black and Tans and the Auxiliaries on the city of Cork, where much of the city centre was burnt down (Source I, page 29).

POLICE NOTICE
£1000 REWARD.
WANTED FOR MURDER IN IRELAND

DANIEL BREEN

(calls himself Commandant of the Third Tipperary Brigade).

Age 27, 5 feet 7 inches in height, bronzed complexion, dark hair (long in front), grey eyes, short cocked nose, stout build, weight about 12 stone, clean shaven; sulky bulldog appearance; looks rather like a blacksmith coming from work; wears cap pulled well down over face.

The above reward will be paid by the Irish Authorities, to any person not in the Public Service who may give information resulting in his arrest.

Information to be given at any Police Station.

Daniel Breen

▼ Born 1894 in County Tipperary, one of eight children
▼ He left school at fourteen to work for local farmers
▼ 1913 he joined the Irish Republican Brotherhood
▼ 1919 became a wanted man with a £1000 price on his head
▼ 1922 elected to the Dail
▼ Died 1969

Dan Breen was typical of the many young Nationalists who fought in the guerrilla war against Britain in 1919–1921. He was always on the run, yet never captured. Most of Breen's exploits took place in 1919. First he took part in the attack on an explosives cart which resulted in the deaths of two policemen and the military occupation of South Tipperary. After this raid, Breen had a £1000 reward offered for his capture. He was severely injured later in the same year whilst releasing his comrade Sean Hogan from police custody. Once again, two policemen died. In November he and others made an attempt on the life of Lord French, the Viceroy of Ireland. The assassination very nearly succeeded. In 1920 his friend Sean Treacy was killed by the British in the middle of Dublin.

Breen rose to become Commandant of the Third Tipperary Brigade, IRA. He met Mahatma Gandhi in London; and was also offered a large sum of money to fight for the Moroccan Nationalists against their Spanish rulers.

Breen rejected the Treaty of 1921 and fought with the Republicans.

As one of your comrades, I state emphatically that I would never have handled a gun or fired a shot, nor would I have asked any of my comrades, many of whom fell on the battlefield, to raise a hand to secure this Treaty.

From Dan Breen's open letter to Sean McKeon, 1921.

He was arrested by the Irish Free State army and, whilst in prison and on hunger strike in 1922, Breen was elected to the Dail as Deputy for Tipperary. Dan Breen represented Tipperary until he retired from politics in 1965.

The Auxiliaries and the Black and Tans poured into Cork, looting, wrecking, drinking, and burning to such effect that a large part of the city centre was completely destroyed, while the fire brigade was deliberately obstructed as they sought to bring the flames under control... The Auxiliaries made their own comment on the affair when they swaggered about the streets of Dublin with burnt corks in their caps.

From *Ireland since the famine* by F. Lyons published in 1973.

i   Ireland is to be called the Irish Free State and is to become a member of the Commonwealth.
ii Irish MPs will have to swear an oath of allegiance to the King.
iii Northern Ireland is to be given the opportunity to remain part of the United Kingdom.
iv The British army is to be removed.
v   Britain is to have three naval bases at Cobh, Berehaven and Lough Swilly.
vi A Boundary Commission will decide on the exact borders between the North and South.

A summary of the terms of the Anglo-Irish Treaty, 1921.

Lloyd George and the British Government were unable to defeat the IRA and were unable to find a solution. The *Government of Ireland Act* of 1920 had failed miserably. By this Act, two Parliaments were suggested for Northern and Southern Ireland, and proportional representation would be used to safeguard the rights of the minorities. Lloyd George accepted that Northern Ireland would be made up of six counties in Ulster which had majority Protestant populations. The two parts of Ireland would send MPs to Westminster; and the Act also suggested that if both parts agreed, then a common Parliament could be established. The elections were held in the spring of 1920 and, in the North, the Ulster Unionists won 40 of the 52 seats. However, in the South, no elections were contested and 124 Sinn Fein members were returned unopposed out of 128 candidates.

By early 1921, it was becoming clear that the war could not be won by either side. A truce was called to end the fighting in July 1921; and the realisation that Northern Ireland was now separated from the South, made the idea of partition more acceptable. The conference to decide the future of Irish independence was held in London and began in October. The Republican delegation was headed by Michael Collins and Arthur Griffith. The resulting Anglo-Irish Treaty, at last creating an independent Ireland, was signed in December 1921.

In Great Britain it was thought that Lloyd George had solved the 'Irish problem'. However, there was unhappiness in the Dail. People such as de Valera felt that the Treaty had surrendered too much to Britain and openly argued with Collins. The debate in the Dail about whether or not to accept the Treaty lasted more than two weeks. The vote showed that 64 were in favour of accepting the treaty and 57 were opposed to it. De Valera resigned as President and was replaced by Griffith, with Collins as head of the new government.

I am against this Treaty... because it will not end the centuries of conflict between the two nations of Great Britain and Ireland... Does the Dail think that the Irish people have changed so much within the past year or two that they now want to get into the British Empire after seven centuries of fighting?

Eamon de Valera speaking in the Dail, December 1921.

Michael Collins

 Collins in 1922 in the uniform of a General in the Irish Free State army

▼ Born 1890
▼ Joined the Irish Republican Brotherhood in 1916
▼ Captured by the British in the Easter Rising
▼ Elected to Parliament 1918
▼ Commanded the IRA between 1919 and 1921, whilst a member of the Dail and on the run
▼ Chief negotiator with the British in 1921
▼ Leader of the Irish Free State, 1921–22
▼ Killed in an ambush during the Irish Civil War, 1922

Collins was born in County Cork, but lived in London from 1906 to 1916, where he was an office worker. He returned to Ireland to take part in the Easter Rising of 1916, when he was captured and held prisoner by the British. After his release, he became one of the chief organisers of the IRA. His exploits became legendary. He personally masterminded the IRA's guerrilla war against the British whilst Finance Minister in the Dail. He also managed to work as the Secretary of the National Aid Association (a fund for IRA widows). All this he did whilst a wanted man, on the run from the Police and their special agents. Collins lived and worked in Dublin, riding his bicycle around the city under the noses of the British. On one occasion he even managed to gain entry into Dublin Castle, the British HQ, in order to read what the British knew about him!

When he found out that the British security forces were very close to discovering his identity and those of his colleagues, he ordered the murder of 12 British secret servicemen. This was known as 'Bloody Sunday' (see pages 27 and 50). Collins personally issued the orders for a number of assassinations, amongst them the killing of Sir Henry Wilson in London in 1922.

In 1921 Collins was sent to Britain to negotiate a Treaty with Lloyd George and Winston Churchill. After one of their meetings, Churchill is reported to have said 'Collins looked as if he was about to shoot me'.

After he brought the Treaty back to Ireland, Collins became the leader of the Free State and Commander-in-Chief of its army in the Civil War against de Valera's Republicans. He died in 1922 when he was shot in the head in an IRA ambush in County Cork.

The pro-Treaty group led by Collins won a convincing majority in the general election of June 1922, but this only spurred de Valera and the anti-Treaty group to challenge the authority of Collins and his Government. Fighting broke out between de Valera's supporters (calling themselves Irregulars or Republicans) and Collins' new Free State army in June 1922. There followed a bloody Civil War until May the following year. Collins, himself, became a victim of the bloodshed, when he was killed in an ambush in August 1922. The Free State Government imprisoned more than 11,000 Republicans and executed 77 during the Civil War. (The number of executions was three times more than the British had carried out during the years 1919–1921.)

The Irish Free State settled to an uneasy relationship with Great Britain, and was determined to amend the Anglo-Irish Treaty as soon as it was possible. There was an uneasy peace within the Free State too, because there were many Republicans who felt that Ulster should never have been allowed to remain within the United Kingdom. The uneasy peace in Ireland was to last almost fifty years, and when the unrest came, it did so in Northern Ireland.

Pro-Treaty Free State soldiers shell anti-Treaty Republicans in their headquarters at the Four Courts in Dublin, July 1922

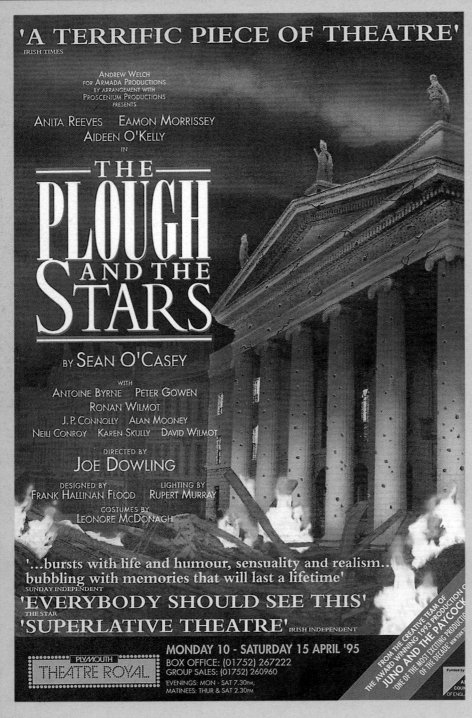

A

A poster advertising a modern production of a play by Sean O'Casey about the Easter Rising

As well as in history books, Irish history has been preserved in art, literature, song, and theatre. But how objective are these interpretations of the events?

B

See who comes over the red-blossomed heather,
Green banners kissing the pure mountain air,
Heads erect! Eyes to front! Stepping proudly together,
Out and make way for the bold Fenian men.
And those who inherit their name and their spirit
Will march with the banners of liberty then
All who love foreign law, native or Sassenach,
Must out and make way for the bold Fenian men.

A traditional Irish folk song which praises the Fenians.

C

For I'm sick to death of slavery
From the day that I was born,
So I'm off to join the IRA
And I'm off tomorrow morn.

We're all off to Dublin in the Green, in the Green...

A folk song about the Easter Rising of 1916.

D

In 1996, the film *Michael Collins*, staring Liam Neeson, had its cinema premier. The film was a box office success, but questions were asked about the accuracy of some of the scenes, such as the armoured car inside Croke Park on Bloody Sunday and the death of Collins' friend Harry Boland.

From a newspaper review article, 1996.

A painting by Sean Keating, 1920. It shows IRA men during the Irish War of Independence, and is called 'Men of the South'.

A still from the film *Michael Collins*, 1996

1 Why do you think plays such as the one featured in Source A still attract large audiences?
2 How accurate an interpretation of the events are songs like those in Sources B and C likely to give?
3 Are they of any use to historians?
4 Study Source D and the film still. Does this source provide evidence that the makers of the film *Michael Collins* got the facts wrong?
5 How does this affect the way an historian might use the film as evidence?
6 How has Keating chosen to portray the IRA men in Source E?
7 How does this affect the way an historian might use this source? Explain your answer.

The Republican family tree

Continuity Army Council. Formed after the 1994 IRA cease-fire, with the intention of continuing the armed struggle.

Modern Sinn Fein. Led by Gerry Adams, this group denies strong links with the IRA and has negotiated with the British Government, the SDLP, and some Ulster Unionists.

Social Democratic and Labour Party. Formed in 1970 as a peaceful alternative to the IRA. Led by John Hume.

The Provisional IRA. A break away group formed in 1969 to carry on the bombing campaign against the British. In 1985 some of its members entered politics as members of the Sinn Fein Party.

Sinn Fein/IRA, the remnants of the Republican fighters once both the Free State (Finne Gael) and de Valera's party (Fianna Fáil) had left them.

Fianna Fáil a break away group of Sinn Fein led by Eamon de Valera. Fianna Fáil re-entered Irish politics in 1926.

The Irish Republican Army (IRA). Between 1919–1921 the Irish Volunteers and what was left of the Irish Citizen Army became the IRA. Organised by Michael Collins, they fought in the Irish War of Independence against the British.

The Irish National Liberation Army. Formed in 1975. Break away group determined to carry on the war against Britain.

Finne Gael (the United Irish Party), the group who remained loyal to Collins and Griffith in 1922. After the Civil War William Cosgrave became their first leader.

Irish Volunteers. A volunteer army raised to defend Irish Home Rule.

Sinn Fein (We Ourselves). A Republican Party formed in 1905 by Arthur Griffith.

The Irish Republican Brotherhood. Republican para-military organisation with as many as 52,000 members in 1889. Its influence declined in the 1890s as people turned towards political movements, though it kept its traditional links with Republicans in the USA. In 1913 it organised the Irish Volunteers

Irish Citizen Army. Formed in November 1913 by the leaders of the Irish Transport Workers Union, Larkin and Connolly. Connolly led the Citizen Army in the Easter rising of 1916 (see page 22)

Cumann na Gaedheal (the Society of Gaels) formed by Arthur Griffith in 1900. This developed into Sinn Fein

The Fenian movement. Formed in 1858 in the USA and named 'Fenians' by John O'Mahony, the movement began to flourish under the same name in Ireland after 1861. It was led at first by James Stephens and later by O'Donovan Rossa. Eventually transformed itself into The Irish Republican Brotherhood.

The United Irishmen, led by Wolfe Tone in 1789.

5 *A*n uneasy truce, 1922–1968

The partition of Ireland was seen as a political success for Lloyd George. He expected that the new province of Northern Ireland would be unable to sustain itself and would be absorbed into the Irish Free State. He was wrong.

The Civil War in the Irish Free State was unexpected, and the divisions which occurred between Collins and de Valera allowed some members of the IRA to continue the fight for a united Ireland long after the Irish politicians had seen the need to accept peace with Britain.

The Irish Free State after 1922

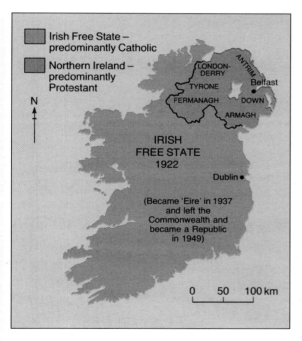

of a united Ireland should still be fought for. In early 1939, the decision was taken to attack mainland Britain and try to disrupt business and communications. There were several incidents and the worst happened in Coventry on 25 August 1939, when five people were killed and 70 were injured. The campaign soon petered out and, by 1945, the IRA was regarded as a spent force. It had lost men in the fighting, had no real funds, and had had many of its members imprisoned without trial. However, there was a resurgence in the 1950s when 'Operation Harvest' was begun. This was a campaign of violence started after the Anti-Partition Movement failed to make any progress. This campaign was called off in 1962 because there was little support in either The Irish Republic or Northern Ireland.

An armed Royal Ulster Constabulary (RUC) policeman stands next to a poster about the murder of a fellow policeman in renewed IRA violence in 1957

There was gradual dilution of the Anglo-Irish Treaty and, by 1949, the following changes had occurred:
i   A new constitution was drawn up in 1937, which was designed for the whole of Ireland.
ii The Irish Free State was renamed Eire in 1937.
iii Britain gave back control of the three naval bases in 1938.
iv Eire finally separated from the British Commonwealth in 1949.

In spite of these changes there were some members of the IRA who felt that the goal

Eamon de Valera

Eamon de Valera is to some people the hero of Irish independence. He was one of the Easter rebels, the leader of the Dail in 1918, the Prime Minister, and the President of Ireland.

To others he is a villain who deliberately wasted opportunities to further Ireland's cause.

▼ Born 1882 in New York, USA
▼ Educated in Dublin
▼ Led a group of rebels during the Easter Rising, and was taken prisoner
▼ Elected to the British Parliament in 1917, but refused to take his seat
▼ Led Republicans in the Civil War of 1922–23
▼ Taoiseach (Prime Minister) of Ireland 1932–48 and 1951–54
▼ President 1959–73
▼ Died in 1975

De Valera's American birth saved his life in 1916, when he escaped the death penalty for his part in the Easter Rising. Between 1916 and 1919 he was arrested and imprisoned twice, escaping to the USA in 1919. In 1921 he was President of the Irish Government in Exile, but refused to represent Ireland in the London talks. Instead he sent Michael Collins and Arthur Griffith to head the talks with the British. De Valera then resigned as he would not accept the Treaty Collins came home with. This split within the Republican movement led to the Civil War of 1922–23.

De Valera re-entered Irish politics in 1926 when he led a break away group of Sinn Fein called Fianna Fáil. In 1932 he became the Prime Minister of Ireland. Later, under a new Constitution, links with the United Kingdom were completely severed. He went on to become President of the Irish Republic. De Valera died in Dublin at the age of 93, two years after retiring from public life.

▶

Eamon de Valera taking the salute from Republican troops during the Irish Civil War, 1922–23. Shortly afterwards he was arrested by the Free State forces.

During the negotiations with the British in 1921, de Valera decided to stay in Ireland and let other, less experienced politicians, talk with Lloyd George and Churchill. Yet he insisted on interfering in their negotiations.

There can be no question of our asking the Irish people to enter an arrangement which could make them subject to the Crown, or demand from them allegiance to the British King. If war is the alternative we can only face it.

De Valera writing to the Irish negotiators in London in 1921.

De Valera's own statements at this time are confusing and contradictory. At the same time as he wrote to the negotiators in London, he met General Smuts, the leader of South Africa.

If the status of a Dominion is offered to me, I will use all our machinery to get the Irish people to accept it.

De Valera speaking to Smuts in 1921.

Many have criticised de Valera for his action, but others support his stance.

Only de Valera at the head of the Irish delegation might have been a match for Lloyd George, but he decided not to go. His enemies have said that it was because he knew there must be a compromise that would attract such outrage among Republicans in Ireland that he did not want to be tarnished by it.

A British historian writing in 1972.

It was indeed because de Valera knew there must be compromise that he stayed in Ireland, but not in his own self interest. By staying in Ireland he was well positioned for the game of bluff necessary to get an acceptable compromise from Lloyd George. He could play the game of being the inflexible Republican. Second, by staying in Ireland he was ready to deal with the delicate political position that would arise at home when news of the compromise broke out.

Adapted from Robert Kee's book *The Green Flag*. Kee is a British author and journalist.

De Valera decided to join the irregular IRA Republicans who fought against the Treaty and the Free State in the Civil War of 1922-3. When he came back to political power in 1932, de Valera began to introduce a number of important measures.

He introduced a new Constitution in 1937 which called for a united Ireland and said Northern Ireland had no right to exist. The Irish Free State was renamed 'Eire'.
He began cutting all economic and political ties with Britain. Imports were cut back, Ireland stayed neutral in the Second World War, the British King was replaced as Head of State by an Irish President.
De Valera introduced a number of laws which favoured the Catholic Church and the Irish Gaelic language.

De Valera's measures when in power.

We shall continue to deny the right of any foreign authority in Ireland. We shall refuse to admit that our country may be carved up by such an authority.

Eamon de Valera, speaking when he was Taoiseach (Prime Minister) of Ireland.

It was de Valera's desire for a united Ireland that made him reject the 1921 Treaty. Then in 1940, during the Second World War, Winston Churchill offered de Valera a united Ireland on condition that British warships could use Irish ports. De Valera rejected the plan.

We are unable to accept the plan. The plan would involve our entry into the war. Our people would be quite unprepared for it. The plan gives no guarantee that in the end we would have a united Ireland. Lord Craigavon (William Craig, the Prime Minister of Northern Ireland) could prevent unification by demanding concessions to which the majority of Irish people could not agree.

Eamon de Valera to the British Government, 1940.

There are even differences in interpretations about de Valera and the withdrawal of Ireland from the British Commonwealth in 1949. De Valera was temporarily out of power in 1949, but had played a leading role in defining Ireland's position regarding the Commonwealth. Any decision to leave the Commonwealth was made before 1949. Therefore, in his book *Conflict in Ireland*, Tony McAleavy states that: 'in 1949 [when de Valera was out of power] the Irish Republic was proclaimed and the country left the British Commonwealth'. He lists this as one of the achievements of de Valera.

This view is contested by Fintan O'Toole, an Irish journalist.

There is good reason to believe that Eamon de Valera, for many the embodiment of hardline Irish Republicanism, wanted to stay in. In 1953 Winston Churchill asked de Valera, 'If you had remained Head of the Irish Government, would you have taken the country out of the Commonwealth?' De Valera's answer was a firm 'No'.

Fintan O'Toole, writing in 1997.

1 Explain how Sources A and B contradict each other.
2 What are the differences in interpretation of de Valera given in Sources C and D?
3 How do you account for these differences?
4 Why did de Valera reject Churchill's offer of a united Ireland?
5 In what ways do Tony McAleavy and Fintan O'Toole interpret de Valera differently?
6 How could you establish which interpretation is the more valid?
7 Considering all the evidence, do you think Eamon de Valera was a hero or a villain? Explain your thoughts fully.

Northern Ireland: What is it all about?

Nationalism.

The Irish Nationalists want a united Ireland, independent from British rule. They are sometimes called Republicans and most of them are Catholic.

My aim was to break the connection with England and win independence.

Theobald Wolfe Tone, 1789.

Ireland unfree shall never be at peace.

Patrick Pearse, 1915.

I still stand by our old principle of complete separation and entire independence.

Dan Breen, 1921.

It is up to this generation of Irish men and women to receive for all time our unity, independence, and freedom.

IRA statement, 1956.

We accept that the Irish people as a whole have a right to national self-determination. This is a view shared by a majority of the people of this island.

Gerry Adams and John Hume, 1993.

Unionism.

The Ulster Unionists want to keep Northern Ireland separate from the Irish Republic and linked to Britain. They are sometimes called Loyalists and most of them are Protestant.

We must be prepared to become responsible for the government of the Protestant Province of Ulster.

Sir Edward Carson, 1911.

I will never give in to any re-arrangement of the boundary that leaves our Ulster area less than it is.

James Craig, 1922.

This country is as determined as in the past to remain part of the United Kingdom.

Basil Brooke, Unionist Prime Minister of Northern Ireland, 1943–1963.

How can I keep Ulster Protestant, loyal, and British?

From the Orange Order, 1966.

Mrs Thatcher tells us that the Republic has got a say in this Province. We say never, never, never, never.

Ian Paisley, 1985.

Northern Ireland after 1922

B Specials in Northern Ireland taking cover during ambush training in April 1922

The Northern Ireland Parliament opened in June 1921, and it was soon clear that the Unionist MPs would be unwilling to sever their links with the United Kingdom. Measures were taken to ensure Unionist control, and thereby Protestant control, in Ulster. The police (the Royal Ulster Constabulary) were allowed to recruit extra forces to maintain security, and these men were known as the B Specials. Some were ex-Ulster Volunteer Force (UVF) and treated Catholic civilians harshly. Over the years they came to be hated by the Catholics.

Politically, Ulster would always send a majority of Protestant MPs to Westminster, and there would always be a majority of Unionist MPs in the Northern Ireland parliament. However, control was also established in local councils, even when the Protestants were in a minority. The vote was restricted to householders and property owners (thus ruling out many of the Catholic poor). Boundaries were redrawn to secure the maximum possible number of Unionist councillors. This process was called 'gerrymandering'.

The use of the gerrymander in Derry, giving a Protestant majority on the Council with a minority of Protestant voters

In 1966 the adult population of Derry was 30 376 (20 102 Catholics; 10 274 Protestants)

More Protestants than Catholics became boundary commissioners because Catholics refused. Therefore, the boundaries of the constituencies favoured Protestants

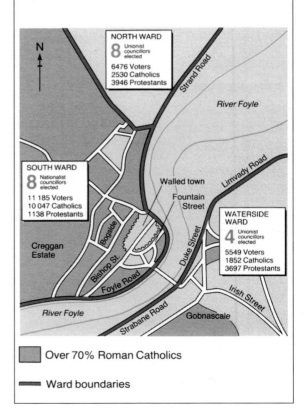

NORTH WARD
8 Unionist councillors elected
6476 Voters
2530 Catholics
3946 Protestants

SOUTH WARD
8 Nationalist councillors elected
11 185 Voters
10 047 Catholics
1138 Protestants

WATERSIDE WARD
4 Unionist councillors elected
5549 Voters
1852 Catholics
3697 Protestants

Over 70% Roman Catholics

Ward boundaries

The results of gerrymandering meant that Unionist councils favoured Protestants over employment and the allocation of council housing. Over the years, it became clear to the Catholics in Northern Ireland that they could not improve their living conditions. It was in the early 1960s that the first attempts were made to put right the injustices created by gerrymandering. In 1963, the Homeless Citizens' League was formed, and this developed into the Campaign for Social Justice. In that same year, the new Prime Minister of Northern Ireland, Terence O'Neill, promised that there would be reforms which would help the Catholics. The reforms were slow to come, and, amidst massive unrest in Europe and the USA, the Northern Ireland Civil Rights Association was formed.

i	One man one vote in local elections
ii	Abolition of gerrymandering
iii	Creation of laws to prevent discrimination by local government
iv	Abolition of the B Specials
v	Allocation of housing on a points basis

Aims of the NICRA.

What had emerged in Northern Ireland was a movement which was based on securing equality of Civil Rights. There were many young people involved in the Civil Rights activities, and they were a product of the improved educational opportunities which were available to the citizens of the United Kingdom in the years after the Second World War.

However, the attempts by O'Neill to improve relations between the two communities were seen by some Protestants as threatening their supremacy. There was a revival of the Orange Order in the 1960s, and the UVF was secretly re-established. Catholic buildings were attacked and several Catholics were murdered in 1966.

Terence O'Neill, Prime Minister of Northern Ireland, dressed in the uniform of the Orange Order

The first Civil Rights march took place in August 1968, and the rally was peaceful with the marchers singing 'We shall overcome', the song that became the anthem of the Civil Rights campaign. However, there was confrontation in the march in Derry on 5 October that year.

Television cameras recorded the scene as police officers drew batons and charged the crowd, laying into them without provocation. The Cameron Commission laid the blame squarely at the feet of the police. Suddenly, Northern Ireland was front page news. The genie was out of the bottle and there was no putting it back.

From *Provos* by P. Taylor, 1997

The 'Troubles' had started.

1 Look at Source B.
Work out the total number of Catholic voters and Protestant voters in Derry. Now work out the total number of Nationalist councillors and the total number of Unionist councillors. What do you notice?

6 The 'Troubles', 1968–1994

Poor housing, unemployment, demand for the vote, and Civil Rights in general were the issues which had let the 'genie out of the bottle' in 1968. This chapter examines how the demand for Civil Rights became a conflict which has seen the death of almost 4,000 people; and one which has its place firmly on the international agenda.

Following the violence of the October 1968 Civil Rights March in Derry, two new groups emerged. The Derry Citizens' Action Committee, led by John Hume (see page 59), and People's Democracy, one of whose leaders was Bernadette Devlin (now McAliskey). People's Democracy were mainly students from Queen's University, Belfast and they organised a march from Belfast to Derry to take place in early January 1969. There were riots in Derry before the marchers had even left Belfast, because the Reverend Ian Paisley (see page 58) had provoked the Protestants by whipping up feelings against the marchers. Protestants were urged to confront the marchers when they reached Burntollet on the outskirts of Derry.

Note:
Catholics in Northern Ireland call this town 'Derry' and Protestants call it 'Londonderry'.

At Burntollet, the police and B Specials took little action to protect the Civil Rights marchers, and some of them even joined in in attacking the marchers in Derry when they eventually reached the city. The British Government later established the Cameron Commission to investigate this violence (Source C).

We refused to accept the politicians' logic that the problems could be seen in terms of Catholic versus Protestant... The crowd at that... Civil Rights march was interested in people's needs.

Bernadette Devlin explaining in her autobiography why the students demonstrated in January 1969. From *The Price of my Soul* by Bernadette Devlin, 1969.

Our investigations have led us to the unhesitating conclusion that on the night of 4-5 January, a number of policemen were guilty of misconduct which involved assault and battery, malicious damage to property in the streets in the mostly Catholic Bogside area... and the use of provocative and sectarian and political slogans.

From the *Cameron Report* on the violence at Burntollet and Derry.

A

Then the marchers came to Burntollet Bridge. From the lanes at each side of the road burst hordes of screaming people wielding bottles, iron bars, cudgels studded with nails. They waded into the march beating hell out of everybody.

I saw a young fellow getting a thrashing from four or five of Ian Paisley's supporters (see page 58) with a policeman looking on. I went rampaging up the road saying not one policeman at Burntollet Bridge would live to be sorry for what he had done.

Bernadette Devlin writing about the fighting at Burntollet.

Bernadette Devlin

Bernadette Devlin was born and brought up in the Catholic area of Dungannon. She attended a Catholic grammar school, where she was educated by nuns. In Source A she describes her education in the 1960s.

St Patrick's Academy was a patriotic school. It owed its proudly Irish slant to the Vice-Principal, Mother Benignus. She disliked the English. All her family had suffered at the hands of the British forces. She was very keen about Irish culture. She didn't hate Protestants. But her view was that you couldn't very well put up with them. They weren't Irish.

We learned Irish history. The interpretations were different from Protestant history books.

Extract from *The Price of my Soul*, Bernadette Devlin, 1969.

In the troubles of 1968 and 1969 Devlin became a leading member of the Civil Rights Movement.

At the age of 21 Bernadette Devlin became the youngest woman to enter the House of Commons, when she won the mid-Ulster by-election.

In Parliament she was outspoken and controversial. During a debate in Parliament following the Bloody Sunday shootings of 1972 (see page 49), Devlin called a Conservative MP a 'murdering hypocrite', pulled his hair and slapped him across the face. In a later debate she menaced Government Ministers with a brown paper bag which she said contained a 'mace' that had been used on the Catholic protestors. Two Ministers dived under a table as Devlin began to tear open the bag and pull out of it a piece of wood into which nails had been hammered.

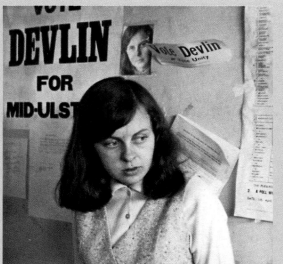

 Bernadette Devlin surrounded by her election posters

1 What did Devlin mean when she wrote, 'we learned Irish history. The interpretations were different from Protestant history books'?
2 How might Devlin's upbringing and education have affected her politics?

E

During the riots in Derry in August 1969, Bernadette Devlin smashes rocks behind the barricades to help the stone throwers. During this riot, she used a microphone to shout to the crowd: 'For God's sake, are you's men at the back just goin' to stand there and leave it to the lads up front? For God's sake, break up the bricks and help them, or are you's all goin' to just stand there, then?' For this act she was sentenced to six months in prison.

The Catholics in Derry's Bogside area built barricades to protect themselves in early 1969. They now felt that they could expect no protection from the police. The situation continued to deteriorate in the following months, with some terrorist explosions which damaged electricity and water supplies to Belfast. The explosions were blamed on the IRA, but, in reality, they were the work of the Ulster Protestant Volunteers, who were trying to discredit the Catholics. The Prime Minister of Northern Ireland, Terence O'Neill, resigned in April 1969, after the general election, when it became clear that there were many who opposed his attempts to bring reforms. The Unionists felt that he was giving in to the Civil Rights groups.

It is worthwhile noting here that Bernadette Devlin was elected as a Member of Parliament at Westminster in April 1969 and that her maiden speech was devastating.

The question before this House, in view of the apathy, neglect and lack of understanding which this House has shown to these people in Ulster whom it claims to represent, is how in the shortest space of time, it can make up for fifty years of neglect, apathy and lack of understanding. Short of producing miracles such as factories overnight in practically every area of Northern Ireland, what can we do? If British troops are sent in I should not like to be either the mother or sister of an unfortunate soldier stationed there.

From *Hansard* (the official record of speeches made in Parliament), April 1969.

The Protestant Orange marches sparked off further trouble in July 1969, but it was the march of the Apprentice Boys in Derry during August which brought wholesale violence on to the streets.

The march passed by the Catholic Bogside and the police again became involved in the riots. The rioting and violence escalated and, after two days, Chichester-Clark, the new Prime Minister of Northern Ireland, asked the Government in Westminster to send in troops to restore order. The rioting was covered on television and the event took on the name 'Battle of the Bogside'.

Trouble in Derry sparked off riots in Belfast, where there was extensive use of guns and huge destruction of property. The fear that was created in the towns resulted in massive population movements between August 1969 and February 1973. It has been estimated that some 60,000 people were forced to leave their homes. It was (at that time) the largest enforced movement of people in Europe since 1945.

A Catholic youth throws a home made petrol bomb at police during the Battle of the Bogside, August 1969.

A cartoon published in *The Observer* on 20 August 1969. The original caption reads: 'It's just as well they believe in the same God'.

In order to calm the fears of the Northern Ireland population, Wilson and Chichester-Clark published the Downing Street Declaration on 19 August 1969.

... there shall be full equality of treatment for all citizens. Both Governments have agreed that the momentum of internal reforms should be maintained... every citizen of Northern Ireland is entitled to the same equality of treatment and freedom from discrimination as exists in the rest of the United Kingdom, irrespective of political views or religion.

Extracts from the Downing Street Declaration, 19 August 1969.

When the troops were sent in, they were at first greeted by the Catholic community as their protectors (see Source C , page 52). When the *Hunt Report* was published in October 1969, the idea that the RUC should be disarmed and the B Specials be disbanded was met with disbelief by the Protestants. There were riots in the Protestant Shankill area of Belfast. The army quelled the riots and two Protestants were killed.

The army moved in and battered its way up the Shankill Road with bloodthirsty enthusiasm. In the shooting two Protestants were killed and a dozen wounded. Many others were beaten or kicked unconscious. Who in the Bogside could doubt that at last law and order were being administered impartially?

An extract from *War and an Irish town* by Eamonn McCann, 1993.

Soldiers in protective clothing charge rioters in Belfast in 1970

There have been a number of interpretations to explain why Northern Ireland erupted into violence in 1968; and why British troops were used to keep the peace there.

Were the riots organised by the IRA?

The police view that they had on their hands an armed uprising led by the IRA was incorrect. There is no credible evidence that the IRA planned or organised the disturbances.

From the official report on the riots, 1972.

In 1967 we discovered that we had no movement.

Cathal Goulding, IRA leader.

Was it part of a wider international protest?

The answer lies partly in the situation itself, but also in the rest of the world in 1968. 1968 was the year of the students' revolt. At French Universities in May, students had brought France to a standstill.

From the British Home Secretary, Jim Callaghan, who first used troops in 1969. He wrote this in 1973.

In 1966 a meeting was held to discuss a Civil Rights Movement for Northern Ireland like the one that black citizens of the United States had organised to demand their rights under the leadership of Martin Luther King.

From Robert Kee, a British author and journalist.

Was it a product of the particular situation in Northern Ireland?

Stone throwing at police in Derry during 'The Battle of the Bogside', August 1969

In 1963 the hard line Unionist Prime Minister Basil Brooke was replaced by Terence O'Neill. O'Neill was keen to end unfair treatment of Catholics... but his reforms were too slow in coming.

In 1967 a group of young Catholics got together and set up a Civil Rights Association. From October 1968 they organised a series of protest marches. These marches ended in violence and bloodshed between Catholics and Protestants. The mainly Protestant police took a tough line towards the Civil Rights campaigners.

O'Neill resigned in April 1969, and by August fighting between Catholics and the Protestant police was out of control.

From a British history book 1996.

Neither the IRA nor any Protestant organisation planned the riots. They arose from a complex situation. There were six occasions during these riots when the police were seriously at fault.

From the official report on the riots, 1972.

Did the British Government rush into using troops to keep the peace?

The head of the Royal Ulster Constabulary asked the army to 'come to the assistance' of the police, and General Freeland passed the request on to the Ministry of Defence. On the afternoon of Sunday 24 July 1969, Ministry officials crowded into my tiny drawing room to advise on how we should respond. We decided that we should wait and passed this recommendation onto Jim Callaghan, the Home Secretary...

When I arrived at my office the next day, I received a message from Harold Wilson (the Prime Minister) himself. We had, he said, been quite right not to rush into the momentous decision to send troops on to the streets of Northern Ireland. 'Once we do that, they may be there for weeks', he said.

Adapted from the Memoirs of Roy Hattersley, who was Minister of State at the Ministry of Defence in 1969. The Memoirs were published in 1995.

Backed by the Prime Minister, I continued to resist the Chief Constable's request. But a week later I was told that Bernadette Devlin – not then a Member of Parliament but already famous as the precocious leader of the militant Civil Rights campaigners – wished to speak to me urgently.

She said, in the simplest language, that unless troops were out of their barracks and into Derry City by mid-afternoon, Catholics would be slaughtered. With Bernadette Devlin supporting the Chief Constable, only one decision was possible. I gained Callaghan's approval, signed the Army Board Order and became 'the man who sent the army on to the streets of Northern Ireland.'

From Roy Hattersley's Memoirs, 1995.

Read Sources A to H.

List the evidence for and against each of the following statements:

i The riots were organised by the IRA.
ii 1968 was part of a wider international protest.
iii The riots and the use of troops were a product of the particular situation in Northern Ireland.
iv The British Government rushed into using troops to keep the peace.

What of the IRA in the early days of the 'Troubles'? Its reputation in the summer of 1969 was severely damaged because it had not been able to protect the Catholics. Slogans appeared on the walls in Belfast: 'IRA – I Ran Away'. There were some in the IRA who felt that the policy of uniting Ireland had to be followed, and that, if violence had to be used to achieve that aim, then violence would be used. However, some IRA members wished to re-unite Ireland by peaceful means. Thus a split occurred in the IRA, and those who embarked on a policy of violence called themselves the Provisional IRA. When first established, there were about 30 Provisionals in Belfast, but they soon expanded and became the main force behind Irish Nationalism.

Violence between the communities continued into the 1970s and the first British soldier was killed in February 1971 (Ensign Robert Curtis). As the violence increased, the British Government sent in more troops and, though the situation tended to stabilize, the decision to introduce internment in August 1971 brought renewed terror to the Province. The new Prime Minister of Northern Ireland, Brian Faulkner, was sure that internment (imprisonment without trial) would destroy the power of the terrorists of both communities. He was wrong.

1971	April–July	August–November
Soldiers	4	30
RUC/UDR	0	11
Civilians	4	73

The arrests, some 1600 by December 1971, were nearly all Catholics, and the IRA stepped up its activities. The Protestant reaction to the increase in violence was the formation of a new group – the Ulster Defence Association (UDA).

Deaths in the months before and after internment began

A Provisional IRA checkpoint at the entrance to the Catholic Bogside and Creggan areas in Derry

The internees were ill-treated and there was an official Commission (The Compton Commission) which looked into conditions.

From *The Compton Report*, 1971.

There was widespread outrage against internment and a march was organised to demand the end of this policy. The date fixed was 30 January 1972. Marches had been banned after the introduction of internment, but this one went ahead. The event went off peacefully until crowds gathered at the army barriers, at which point there was some stone throwing and the army responded with water cannon and rubber bullets. As the situation worsened, firing began and soon thirteen civilians lay dead. This was Bloody Sunday. The British army has always maintained that it was fired on first. Marchers have always said that the army fired the first shots.

I was one of 1000 lying flat on their faces as the shooting continued. Pinned to the ground, it was impossible to tell who fired the first shots.

A reporter for *The Daily Telegraph*, 1972.

... personnel carriers approached... paratroopers hurled themselves forward... these men began firing on the crowd and killed thirteen people. Seventeen others were wounded.

From *The Troubles* by T P Coogan, 1996.

There was no general breakdown in army discipline... soldiers who identified armed gunmen fired on them in accordance with the standing orders. At one end of the scale, some soldiers showed a high degree of responsibility, at the other... firing bordered on the reckless.

From *The Widgery Report*, the official British Government investigation into Bloody Sunday.

Friends carry one of the injured marchers through the British lines on Bloody Sunday, escorted by a Catholic priest

Bloody Sunday 21 November 1920; 29 killed

The events

Just after nine o'clock in the morning, twelve British officers were shot dead in their beds or at breakfast. Two Auxiliaries who interfered with one of the shootings were also killed.

In the afternoon, some Auxiliaries and police opened fire on the crowd at a Gaelic football match in Croke Park. Twelve civilians, including a woman, a child, and one of the players were killed.

That night two IRA men and another prisoner were killed by Auxiliaries in Dublin Castle jail.

What had brought about these events?

a Tactical causes. The IRA's main advantage in the war against the British was its undercover agents. The police had brought in a number of intelligence experts from England, who were working with Irish detectives in an attempt to uncover these agents. Michael Collins, the organiser of the IRA (see page 30), had learned that the British secret police possessed details of him and his leading agents.

b Political causes. Collins also thought the time was right to send a firm message to the British Prime Minister, David Lloyd George. Negotiations for a cease-fire had begun. Lloyd George seemed to be gaining confidence; two weeks before Bloody Sunday he had made a speech in which he said he 'had murder by the throat'.

c Poor planning. The heavy policing of the Croke Park football match had been planned days before. But the Auxiliaries who were sent there had lost two of their comrades that morning. Their mood was 'ugly'. It was reported afterwards that the first shots came from the crowd, but this is not proven.

d Revenge. Richard McKee and Peadar Clancy were the IRA men killed in Dublin Castle. They had nothing to do with the assassinations, having been arrested 24 hours before. The authorities say they were shot trying to escape. Their bodies were dumped on the street the next day, riddled with bullets. The third man killed, called Clune, was not even a member of the IRA.

Bloody Sunday 30 January 1972; 13 killed

The events

Catholic Civil Rights marchers were demonstrating in Derry. They were confronted by police and soldiers at the barricades at Free Derry corner. The soldiers were ordered to clear the streets. Soldiers from the Parachute Regiment moved in and began shooting. Some of the crowd flung themselves to the ground, others panicked. Thirteen unarmed men were shot dead.

What had brought about these events?

a The escalation of violence. Soldiers had been attacked by Catholic youths. The occasional brutality from the soldiers had provoked an angry response. In 1970, armed IRA had appeared on the streets to challenge the troops. Soldiers were armed with both rubber bullets and live ammunition.

b Fear. Before January 1972, a number of British soldiers had been killed by gunmen in Northern Ireland. It was said after the events of the day that shots had been heard. If the paratroopers thought they were being shot at by an IRA sniper, it is possible that they may have panicked themselves.

c The Paras. The army was trained and designed to be aggressive, but the Parachute Regiment was one of the toughest in the army. Paratroops were specially selected and trained for difficult operations. They were not trained for crowd control situations.

▲ February 1997, the 25th Anniversary of the second Bloody Sunday. Crowds gather at Free Derry corner and pictures of the victims are spread on the grass.

1 What similarities can you find in the causes of these two events? Are there any differences?
2 Why do you think commemorations like those in the photograph are held?
3 Do you think the Anniversary of the first Bloody Sunday is also commemorated? Give your reasons.

Through the centuries British soldiers have been sent to Ireland by the Government, or have been caught up in the conflict in other ways.

> Cromwell's soldiers promised to spare the lives of any who laid down their arms. But when they had all in their power, the word 'No quarter' went around.

From a letter written by the Marquis of Ormonde in 1649. He was complaining about the conduct of English soldiers after the siege of Drogheda.

> A Belfast docker, John Benson, painted 'No tea here' on the wall of his street. The army complained to the police. Benson was given six months imprisonment.

From *The Sunday Times*, 1972

Belfast, September 1969. Some of the first British soldiers sent to Northern Ireland in 1969 are given cups of tea by a Belfast housewife.

Two Auxiliaries and a British soldier with an RIC policeman in 1921. British troops had been in Ireland since the 1916 Rising. After the First World War, the Auxiliaries and Black and Tans were recruited and sent to Ireland to support the Royal Irish Constabulary.

Horses of the Household Cavalry lie dead in Hyde Park, London, following the explosion of an IRA bomb in 1982

1   Using information from this page, together with the rest of the book, explain how the role of the British army in Ireland has changed.
2   How has the attitude of the Northern Irish to the use of troops changed? Explain your answer.

It was inevitable that the deaths of so many civilians would cause further trouble and, during the subsequent weeks, it appeared to the outside world that law and order was breaking down. The Unionist Party in Northern Ireland split into smaller and more extreme groups. Prime Minister Faulkner no longer had the support of his MPs and there was little he could do. The Westminster Government stepped in. Prime Minister Heath suspended Stormont (the Northern Irish Parliament) and Direct Rule began on 24 March 1972. Many observers have said that Direct Rule came three years too late. If there had been decisive intervention and prompt reform of the grievances highlighted by the Civil Rights demonstrators, then it is possible that the 'Troubles' would not have occurred.

Direct Rule did not seem to improve the situation. By July 1972, there were 21,000 troops in the Province and violence on both sides of the religious divide continued. Reforms were carried out but they were too late – the B Specials were dissolved, gerrymandered boundaries were changed, and a new security force was set up (the Ulster Defence Regiment).

As you can see from the events box on the left, the 1970s and early 1980s were characterised by violence and some attempts to bring peace. The Sunningdale Agreement held out a prospect of some solution, but it collapsed completely in the face of a general strike called by the Ulster Workers' Council. The Women's Peace Movement gained tremendous support and momentum in 1976. A procession of Protestant and Catholic women marched together through both Republican and Loyalist parts of Belfast. The founders, Betty Williams and Mairead Corrigan, were awarded the Nobel Peace Prize in 1977. However, the Movement did not bring peace to the Province.

1972	Birmingham pub bombings: 19 killed, 182 injured
1973	Harrods bombed in London
1973	Sunningdale Agreement, led to power-sharing
1974	Power-sharing collapsed
1974	M62 coach bomb. Guildford pub bombing: 5 killed
1975	Irish National Liberation Army formed (a splinter group from the IRA)
1976	Women's Peace Movement founded by Betty Williams and Mairead Corrigan
1979	Airey Neave MP, Conservative spokesperson for Northern Ireland, killed
1979	Lord Mountbatten killed (15 soldiers also killed on the same day)
1981	Second bout of hunger strikes at the Maze Prison. Bobby Sands and 9 others died
1982	Hyde Park and Regent's Park bombings
1983	Harrods bombing. 38 IRA prisoners escaped from the Maze Prison
1984	Brighton bombing at the Conservative Party Conference. One Conservative MP and 6 leading members of the Party killed.

▶ Rescuers try to release the injured after the Brighton bombing of the Conservative Party Conference, 1984

The IRA varied its tactics in the 1970s by bringing the conflict to the British mainland. There was a series of bombing campaigns aimed mainly at London and Birmingham. There were many casualties and with each successive campaign the IRA became more daring. The year 1979 saw their most devastating action – the killing of Lord Mountbatten, Queen Elizabeth II's uncle. Despite these actions, the British Government continued to state that they would never give in to terrorism.

This was made crystal clear to the IRA when the Maze hunger strikers, led by Bobby Sands, were allowed to die in the quest for special category (i.e. political) prisoner status. Though the IRA called off the hunger strikes, they did not lose support. More than 50,000 people went to the funeral of Bobby Sands and there were always plenty of volunteers in the Maze Prison ready to begin a hunger strike.

 The funeral of Bobby Sands with an IRA honour guard

However, the Government's message may have begun to be appreciated by Sinn Fein, the political wing of the IRA, because in 1981 it announced that it would begin to campaign in local and general elections. Rather menacingly, Sinn Fein said it would 'campaign with a ballot paper in one hand and an Armalite in the other'. The Party had some initial success when Gerry Adams became MP for West Belfast and two years later Sinn Fein had 59 councillors in the Province.

Newspaper reactions to the murder of Lord Mountbatten in 1979

A Wall art on the Falls Road in Belfast in 1981

D

In previous hunger strikes of the period, in Mountjoy jail in 1919 and in Wormwood Scrubs in 1920, the Government had given in after ten days or so, or when the hunger strikers seemed close to death, being unwilling to create martyrs. In the case of Terrance McSwiney, Lord Mayor of Cork, the Government had announced it had no intention of giving in to moral blackmail.

On 24 October 1920, after a 73 day hunger strike, McSwiney died. Another IRA hunger striker died in Cork prison a few hours later.

Adapted from *The Green Flag* by Robert Kee, 1972.

E

When Gandhi returned to politics in 1939, his first act was to undertake a fast (hunger strike) to force the ruler of Rajkot to change his autocratic rule. The public unrest was so great that Gandhi's demands were granted. In 1948, when India was at war with itself and thousands were being killed, he went on hunger strike again to stop the people fighting.

From an American history book written in 1995. It is commenting on the hunger strikes undertaken by the Indian leader, Gandhi.

You have read about the causes of the hunger strikes; and about the deaths of Bobby Sands and 9 other prisoners. Why did these prisoners decide on hunger strikes as a form of protest? Hunger striking had a long tradition by 1981, both inside and outside Ireland.

B

They push a tube up the nostril which goes wriggling down into the stomach. Then there's a funnel on the end of the tube which they pour the water and food in, you see.

All the time they were pushing this bally tube down, I kept coughing and coughing incessantly. Well, I didn't know what was the matter, but I understand it was double pneumonia and pleurisy, due to food getting into my lungs.

Emmeline Pankhurst, the leader of the Suffragettes, writing about force feeding of hunger strikers in British prisons, 1914.

C

Now, in my native country, I was a prisoner in the hands of my own countrymen. May the reader never know what it is like to be marched, a prisoner, through his native town for doing what he believed to be his duty in the cause of his country.

I was taken to Mountjoy jail.

In protest at the treatment meted out to me, I went on hunger strike. After twelve days of hunger and six of thirst strike I was released.

From *My Fight for Irish Freedom* by Daniel Breen, 1924.

1 How does the evidence in this feature help you to explain why the hunger strike was started in 1981?
2 The wall painting (Source A) says 'Blessed are those who hunger for justice'. What evidence can you find in Sources B–E that previous hunger strikers were campaigning for justice?
3 The phrase 'Blessed are those who hunger for justice' is one interpretation of events in the Maze prison in 1981. How might
   a the Ulster Unionist, Ian Paisley (page 58), and
   b the British Prime Minister in 1981, Margaret Thatcher, have interpreted the Maze hunger strikes?

More than many modern world issues, Northern Ireland has seen women at the forefront of activities. In 1916 Constance Markievicz, the first woman MP, was active during the Easter Rising and became a member of the Dail government (see page 26). In 1968 Bernadette Devlin led the Civil Rights Movement and later became an MP (see page 43).

Mairead Corrigan and Betty Williams, the Peace Marchers, with Jane Ewart-Biggs (centre), the wife of the murdered British Ambassador to Ireland

Two women, Mairead Corrigan and Betty Williams, began the Women's Peace Movement. They staged rallies and marches for peace which caught the imagination of both the Catholic and Protestant communities. They won the Nobel Peace Prize in 1997.

When Bobby Sands died, many of us felt it's back to square one. If you tried to call a peace rally now you wouldn't get anyone to come. There is far more bitterness and a feeling of anti-Britishness.

Mairead Corrigan, the peace campaigner, speaking in 1981.

In November 1985, Margaret Thatcher, the first woman to become the Prime Minister of Britain, made a breakthrough when she signed the Anglo-Irish Agreement.

Margaret Thatcher and Garret Fitzgerald, the Irish Prime Minister, exchange documents after signing the Anglo-Irish Agreement in Belfast

Some progress about the future of Ireland was made in 1985, when the British and Irish governments drew up the Accord (also called the Anglo-Irish Agreement). The British and Irish Governments were to meet on a regular basis to discuss:

● political matters
● Security
● legal matters, including extradition
● cross-border co-operation between security forces

Both Westminster and the Dail welcomed the Agreement, but the Ulster Unionists did not. They felt that their interests were not being safeguarded. The USA was impressed by the progress that had been made and offered $250 million over five years to help make it work. The Agreement was denounced by the UDA as a sellout, and a new Protestant Action Force emerged. The 15 Ulster Unionist MPs resigned and forced a mini-referendum. The Unionist leaders called for strikes against the Agreement, and as a result of loyalist demonstrations, the British Government was forced to send 500 extra troops to keep order.

1985–6	Libya supplied arms to the IRA
1987	Sinn Fein lost political support in elections
1987	Enniskillen bombing on Remembrance Sunday: 11 killed and 63 injured
1988	SAS killed 3 IRA members in Gibraltar. 2 British army corporals killed when they drove by an IRA funeral. Loyalist gunman killed one IRA member and two mourners at another IRA funeral
1989	10 killed at the Royal Marines Music School, Deal, Kent. UFF murdered several Sinn Fein and IRA members
1990	IRA used 'human bomb' and killed six soldiers and one civilian. Ian Gow MP killed by car bomb
1991	Mortar attack on Downing Street. Bombings at Victoria and Paddington railway stations in London
1992	Baltic Exchange bombing - £800 million worth of damage caused. UFF attack on Belfast bookmakers: 5 Catholics killed
1993	Warrington and Bishopsgate bombings
1996	Canary Wharf bombing. Aldwych bus bomb.

 The funeral cortege of Nurse Marie Wilson, who was one of the 11 people killed in the Enniskillen bombing on Remembrance Sunday 1987, passes the scene of the bomb blast - the town's war memorial

The events box on the left shows that the activities of the Nationalist and Loyalist groups continued to cause misery in the UK. However, despite this, it is in the late 1980s that the beginnings of the 'peace process' can be seen. Sinn Fein altered its political strategy and began to build alliances with other groups, including the SDLP, the Dublin Government, the American President, and Irish America. John Hume of the SDLP and Gerry Adams of Sinn Fein met in 1988. Hume wanted a conference convened by the Irish Government and he wrote to Adams suggesting it.

The conference would try and reach agreement on the exercise of self-determination in Ireland and on how the people of our diverse traditions can live together in peace, harmony and agreement. It would be understood that if this conference were to happen, that the IRA would have ceased its campaign.

From John Hume's letter to Gerry Adams in 1988.

Ian Paisley, wearing the sash of the Orange Order, speaking to a large crowd in Portadown, 1995

▼ Founder of the Democratic Unionist Party in 1971
▼ Forceful and powerful personality
▼ Tough line on IRA, calling for its destruction
▼ MP and MEP (Member of the European Parliament)
▼ Boycotted the peace negotiations in 1997

Ian Paisley became famous as a tough and outspoken Unionist and opponent of the IRA and Irish Nationalism. In 1971 he formed the Democratic Unionist Party, as he believed the 'official' Unionists to be weak. He strongly opposed the 'power-sharing' experiment in 1974.

Catholics do not want a share in the government of Northern Ireland. They want Northern Ireland to be destroyed, and to have a united Ireland. Even if they were to join a government it is only until such time as they can destroy the Government and the State.

Ian Paisley speaking about his reasons for opposing power-sharing in 1974.

These men are ready to fight and die rather than accept an all-Ireland Republic. They are prepared to defend their province in the same way as Lord Carson and the men of the Ulster Volunteer Force!

Ian Paisley speaking about the 500 men from a private Protestant army he was parading around Northern Ireland in 1981.

The ordinary Ulsterman is not going to surrender to the IRA... We have not only the right but the duty to kill them before they kill me, my family and others.

Ian Paisley, 1982.

We pray this night that Thou wouldst deal with the Prime Minister of our country. O God, in wrath take vengeance on this wicked, treacherous lying woman. Take vengeance upon her, O Lord, and grant that we shall see a demonstration of Thy power.

Ian Paisley speaking in his Belfast church, 1985. He was asking God to punish the British Prime Minister, Margaret Thatcher, for signing the Anglo-Irish Agreement.

John Hume

John Hume outside 10 Downing Street after a meeting with the British Prime Minister, John Major, in 1994

▼ Northern Irish Catholic
▼ Leader of the Social Democratic and Labour Party (SDLP), formed in 1970
▼ His election headquarters were bombed by the IRA in 1984
▼ Strong supporter of the 1985 Anglo-Irish Agreement
▼ Made an agreement with Sinn Fein in 1993

For many years John Hume was the spokesman for the non-violent Nationalists of Northern Ireland. In the late 1980s and early 1990s, when there seemed to be a stalemate in Northern Ireland, Hume was secretly meeting with Gerry Adams, the leader of Sinn Fein (see page 74). These talks were focused upon the question of how the Nationalists could adopt a new approach to Northern Irish politics. In 1993 both men informed the Dublin government that they had made substantial progress towards achieving an IRA cease-fire.

However, as has often happened in Irish politics, there was an immediate setback. Eight British soldiers were killed in August 1988 in Tyrone, and three days later the SAS shot dead three IRA men. The British Government then introduced restrictions which stopped all broadcasting organisations from transmitting the actual voices of those believed to be involved in 'terrorism' or organisations that were thought to support it. The idea was 'to starve these groups of the oxygen of publicity'. Nevertheless, the new Secretary of State for Northern Ireland, Peter Brooke, openly stated in 1989 that the British Government might talk to Sinn Fein.

Yet the rollercoaster of violence continued. 1990 was an appalling year:

- 11 civilians killed
- 11 policemen killed
- 18 soldiers killed
- 2 Australian tourists killed in Holland (they were thought to be off duty British soldiers)

Martin McGuinness (left), along with other IRA leaders, gives a press conference in 1972. He was later to become a Sinn Fein MP and one of their chief negotiators.

▼

There was open revulsion against the IRA, and Martin McGuinness said that there was nowhere else to go but the negotiating table. There also seemed to be some cause for optimism with the arrival of a new Prime Minister, John Major, at Downing Street. In addition, there was now some urgency in the situation, because statisticians were pointing out that there would be a Catholic majority in Northern Ireland in just over a generation. Indeed, British policy did seem to be expressed more clearly when Peter Brooke said that Britain 'remained in Northern Ireland because that was the wish of the majority of its population'. But the rollercoaster of sectarian violence continued and the killings in 1991 and 1992 reached shocking proportions. By the end of 1992, for the first time in the history of the 'Troubles', the Loyalist paramilitaries claimed as many victims as the IRA – both having killed 34.

The British Government began secret talks with the IRA in March 1993; and John Hume and Gerry Adams also met at the same time. John Major also had talks with Albert Reynolds, the Prime Minister of The Irish Republic, but could not offer much. Because of his slender majority, he was dependent on the Ulster Unionists for support in Parliament. The tit for tat sectarian killings reached a crescendo at the end of 1993, when the IRA planted a bomb in a fish shop on the Shankill Road, killing ten people. The Loyalists retaliated with the murders of six Catholics in a bar in Greysteel. October 1993 saw 27 civilians killed, making it the highest number of monthly casualties since October 1976.

The breakthrough came in December 1993, following further meetings between Major and Reynolds. The Downing Street Declaration was issued (Source M).

The Declaration was not welcomed wholeheartedly by the Republicans. However, events moved quickly in the New Year. In January 1994, Gerry Adams was given a visa to visit the USA. Adams took America by storm. The visit caused relations between the UK and the USA to deteriorate, and, when further visas were granted and the ban on fund-raising was lifted, there were many in the UK who felt that President Clinton had been duped by Adams. There was no move on the anticipated cease-fire and the death toll continued to rise. The Loyalist UVF carried out an horrific attack in June and killed six men as they watched Ireland playing football in the World Cup.

The IRA finally announced its cease-fire on 31 August 1994.

The Prime Minister, on behalf of the British government, reaffirms that they have no selfish, strategic or economic interest in Northern Ireland. The role of the British Government will be to encourage, facilitate and enable the achievement of agreement. They accept that such agreement may take the form of agreed structures for the *island as a whole*, including a *united Ireland* achieved by peaceful means on the following basis. The British Government agree that it is for the people of the island of Ireland alone, by agreement between the two parts respectively, to exercise their right of self-determination on the basis of consent, freely and concurrently given, North and South, to bring about a united Ireland, if that is their wish.

The Downing Street Declaration of December 1993.

Recognising the potential of the situation and in order to enhance the democratic peace process and underline our commitment to its success, the leadership of Oglaigh na Eireann (IRA) have decided that... there will be a complete cessation of military operations...
We believe that an opportunity to create a just and lasting peace has been created... We note the Downing Street Declaration is not a solution, nor was it presented as such by its authors. A solution can only be found as a result of inclusive negotiations.

Extracts from the IRA press release announcing their cease-fire, August 1994.

The Loyalists announced their own cease-fire on 13 October 1994, on the condition that the IRA maintained theirs.

In many ways the Northern Ireland issue is not confined to the Province. Of course, the politics and violence linked with Northern Ireland have spread to both mainland Britain and the Irish Republic. However, there are also links with other parts of the world and with other world movements.

The USA and the Irish issue

The Irish issue has always been important in the USA because of the enormous numbers of Irish people who migrated to the USA, beginning in the mid-nineteenth century.

In 1859 the Fenian Brotherhood (see page 34) was formed in the USA by James Stephens and John O'Mahony. By 1865 O'Mahoney was able to collect $250,000 from the USA to use in Ireland. The American newspapers carried advertisements for money to equip Irish ships to 'hoist the Green flag and sweep English commerce from the seas.'

Up to and during the First World War, support for the Irish position was so strong (see Source A) that cartoons such as Source B were published to counter it.

There is not an Irishman in America today who would not rejoice to hear that a German army was marching in triumph across England.

From an American newspaper, 1908.

WHAT AMERICA THINKS
(CARTOON FROM THE NEW YORK "LIFE.")

Uncle Sam — WHEN YOU STAB HIM YOU STAB ME, AND THIS IS A GOOD TIME TO REMEMBER THE FACT.

In 1919 Eamon de Valera (see pages 36–8) sailed to the USA to try to gain support for the Irish rebellion against British rule.

The American organisation, Noraid, managed to raise £ 4 million for the IRA in the 1970s-1980s. Noraid also helped the IRA by buying and transporting US Armalite machine guns for use in Northern Ireland.

At the time of the hunger strikes in the early 1980s, many Irish Americans sympathised with the Nationalists in Northern Ireland and protested against British measures.

Protesters in New York, USA. They are burning a Union Jack outside the British Consulate, in protest at the death of hunger striker Bobby Sands in 1981 (see page 54).

C

Eamon de Valera giving a speech in Los Angeles, USA in 1919

In the mid 1990s US President Bill Clinton put pressure on both sides in the Northern Ireland conflict. He promised US economic help for Ireland and invited the Sinn Fein leader, Gerry Adams, to visit the USA. After the 1994 cease-fire, Clinton visited Belfast to express his support for the peace process.

Northern Ireland and European co-operation

Both John Hume and Ian Paisley are elected Members of the European Parliament, which sits in Brussels and Strasbourg. The European Union granted £230 million to Northern Ireland and the border counties of the Irish Republic. This money was to encourage reconciliation projects. In 1997 Mark Byrne, a young journalist with the European Youth Parliament, asked Gerry Adams about Sinn Fein's attitude towards Europe.

 E

Mark Byrne: Does your Party support the involvement of the European Union in the latest strategies to advance peace in Northern Ireland?

Gerry Adams: Sinn Fein commends the peace and reconciliation funding which has been provided by the EU. The support the EU has given those engaged in efforts for a just and lasting peace is also to be commended.

Mark Byrne: Does your Party support further European integration, or is it 'Eurosceptic'?

Gerry Adams: Sinn Fein has always opposed the formation of a European super state. We believe the EU is an alliance of the rich industrial powers, which have formed a bloc to advance their own interests against those of the poorer countries. Sinn Fein is opposed to a Single European Currency on the basis that a national currency is needed for national independence.

Another problem is the erosion of Irish neutrality through participation in the common foreign and security policy. Sinn Fein will be in the lead of any campaigns opposed to the further erosion of national sovereignty by the EU.

From an interview with Gerry Adams, 1997.

The effect of world events on Northern Ireland

Both the American and French Revolutions in the late 1700s probably had some effect on the Rebellion of the United Irishmen under Theobald Wolfe Tone in 1798.

You have seen on page 46 how the events in the USA and France in 1967-1968 may have contributed to both the Civil Rights Movement and the riots in Northern Ireland.

In addition to this, other independence movements around the world may have had an effect on the development of the IRA.

 F A wall painting in Northern Ireland. It links the aims of the IRA with the Palestinian Liberation Organisation (PLO).

The Irish Republican Army has developed some links with other similar groups. It is difficult to know how strong these links have ever been, but it seems likely that members of the IRA have met and trained with terrorists from other armed groups who are fighting for their national independence.

1 Using the information and sources in this feature, explain how events and movements outside Britain and Ireland have had an effect on the Northern Ireland conflict.

A

This shows the red hand of Ulster in the badge of the Ulster Freedom Fighters. Painted on Newtownards Road, Belfast.

THEIR ONLY CRIME IS LOYALTY
LPA. LPOW.
WE FORGET THEM NOT

FUF
EAST BELFAST.

FOR AS LONG AS ONE HUNDRED OF US REMAIN ALIVE WE SHALL NEVER IN ANY WAY CONSENT TO SUBMIT TO THE RULE OF THE IRISH FOR ITS NOT FOR GLORY WE FIGHT BUT FOR FREEDOM ALONE WHICH NO MAN LOSES BUT WITH HIS LIFE

A Loyalist painting has been defaced with green paint

B

IN GLORIOUS MEMORY

1916 1990
FREE
IRELAND

Painting large murals on the ends of the terraces of houses has become a way by which both sides in the conflict can have their say about what is happening. They are also a form of urban art and a means of propaganda. These paintings are very large, sometimes beautiful, and take a great deal of time and effort to complete. Here is a small selection of wall paintings for you to examine and think about.

'Who will defend Ulster now?'

'Free Ireland'. Wall art on the Falls Road, Belfast.

1 What events are shown in Source B?
2 Why do you think it has been defaced in this way?

3 Comment on the contents of Source D. When do you think this wall painting was done? Give your reasons.
4 What events is Source E showing? When do you think this painting was completed?

THE IRISH FRANKENSTEIN.

 A

British attitudes to the Irish Republicans. A *Punch* cartoon of 1882 likens the IRB to Frankenstein's monster.

B

The people on this side of the water have seen their sons spat upon and murdered. Who do these people think they are?

British Prime Minister Harold Wilson, 1974.

 C

There is no such thing as political murder, political bombing, or political violence. We will not compromise on this.

British Prime Minister Margaret Thatcher, 1981.

D

British attitudes to the Irish. A *London Evening Standard* cartoon, 1982.

E

Is there anyone here who objects to taking power with a ballot paper in one hand and an Armalite rifle in the other?

Danny Morrison, speaking at a Sinn Fein Conference in 1983.

F

If the British come here and shoot our men and women, the only way is for Irish people to shoot them back. If it takes another 800 years, we'll get them out of the country. There's only one way to send them back – that's in boxes.

Patrick Hill, one of the released Birmingham Six, 1993.

G

The release from prison of the Birmingham Six in 1991. Their life sentences for the Birmingham pub bombings were overturned by the Court of Appeal.

H

The only solution for dealing with the IRA is to kill 600 people in one night.

Alan Clarke, a Conservative politician, speaking at the 1997 Conservative Party Conference.

1   What are the similarities between Sources A and D?
2   What are the similarities between Sources B and C?
3   What are the similarities and differences between Sources F and G?
4   What are the similarities and differences between Sources F and H?
5   These sources cover a period from 1882 to 1997. Taking all of the sources into consideration, do you think there have been any changes in attitude towards the so called 'men of violence' during this period? Explain your answer.

7 *T*he Peace Process, 1994–1997

At last there was a cease-fire. But, as usual, there were those groups who were not completely happy with the news. The IRA had not included the word 'permanent' in their statement, and this omission was crucial for the Unionists.

There is no way the IRA would give up its arms in advance. When I looked around the world, it wasn't a precondition in Bosnia, the Middle East, or indeed in South Africa. Decommissioning was never a precondition.

Albert Reynolds, Prime Minister of The Irish Republic speaking in October 1994.

In March 1995, Sir Patrick Mayhew, Secretary of State for Northern Ireland, set out three conditions for decommissioning, and, if these were met, Sinn Fein could be invited to the all-party talks.

● The IRA had to be willing in principle to disarm progressively.
● It had to agree on how in practise decommissioning would be carried out.
● it had to decommission some of its weaponry at the beginning of the talks as an obvious gesture of good faith.

▲ Newly painted wall art in the Bogside area of Londonderry in August 1994. It was painted to commemorate the 25th Anniversary of the Battle of the Bogside and the deployment of British troops in Northern Ireland. It shows the strength of feeling in Republican areas, despite the IRA cease-fire.

The second major hurdle to be negotiated was the issue of 'decommissioning', or the disarmament of the IRA and Loyalist arsenals. The IRA was unwilling to give up its weapons. It said that in similar situations in the rest of the world, arms were always given up when a final settlement was reached. It was felt that if weapons were given up now, before all-party talks, then the interpretation would be simple – the IRA had surrendered. As far as the IRA was concerned, the issue of decommissioning was not on the agenda and, eventually, the cease-fire ended because agreement could not be reached on this awkward problem.

This third point became known as 'Washington Three' and could not be met by the IRA. Nevertheless, the peace process seemed to move on smoothly when, in November 1995, President Clinton visited Northern Ireland. However, intelligence reports suggested that the IRA was unhappy with the slow progress towards all-party talks, and that some members were prepared to resort to violence once again.

I think also at that stage there was the potential spectre of a split in the movement [IRA]. I have no doubt that the preparations for the Canary Wharf bomb were made in the latter part of 1995.

Hugh Annesley, Chief Constable of the RUC, writing in 1996.

In order to avoid a crisis, John Major and John Bruton (the new Prime Minister of The Irish Republic) agreed on a 'twin track' approach to decommissioning. An international body was set up chaired by former US Senator George Mitchell, accompanied by Harri Holkeri, former Finnish Prime Minister, and General John de Chastelain, Canadian Chief of Defence Staff. The *Mitchell Report* was published on 22 January 1996. The Report wanted a commitment and adherence to fundamental democracy and non-violence, by an acceptance of six principles.

A commitment:
- to democratic and exclusively peaceful means of resolving political issues
- to the total disarmament of all para-military organisations
- to agree that such disarmament must be verifiable to the satisfaction of an independent commission
- to renounce for themselves, and to oppose any effort by others, to use force or threaten to use force, to influence the course of the outcome of all-party negotiations
- to agree to abide by the terms of any agreement reached in all-party negotiations and to resort to democratic and exclusively peaceful methods in trying to alter any aspect of that outcome with which they may disagree
- to urge that 'punishment' killings and beatings stop and to take effective steps to prevent such actions

A summary of the six principles in the *Mitchell Report,* January 1996.

But John Major then alienated Sinn Fein by announcing that elections would be held for a forum that would sit to accompany all-party talks. The result would obviously favour the Loyalists and reflect their majority. The IRA was surprised at this decision, and, on 9 February 1996, Canary Wharf in London's Docklands was bombed. Two people were killed, 100 were injured and damage was estimated at £85 million. Martin McGuinness said that he had no foreknowledge of the bomb and that there was 'considerable danger that the authority of people like himself and Gerry Adams had been undermined'. The cease-fire had lasted for 17 months. Some observers feel that if the IRA had not bombed Docklands, it would probably have split. (It is interesting to note that in November 1997, several leading IRA and Sinn Fein members did quit these organisations because of internal rifts.)

Despite the renewal of violence, the British and Irish Governments pressed ahead with the peace process and announced a firm date for all-party talks – 10 June 1996. Sinn Fein would be allowed to participate if the IRA called another cease-fire. However, the IRA continued its campaign of violence and, in June 1996, a one and a half tonne bomb devastated the centre of Manchester. There were 200 injured and damage was estimated at £100 million.

Violence erupted in Ulster in July 1996, during the marching season, with all attention focussed on Portadown (see pages 70–1). Following the march, sectarian violence and rioting were headline news, and, in the week of the Drumcree march, the RUC fired 6,000 plastic bullets. There were claims by Catholics once more that the RUC had been lenient towards the Protestants in the disturbances.

It is traditional for members of the Orange Order to march in parades each July. They are commemorating the victory of the Protestant King William III at the Battle of the Boyne in 1690. In this battle William defeated the Catholic army of James II. William III is also known as William of Orange. The marchers wear orange sashes and carry banners.

The Catholic population of Northern Ireland feel that these marches are organised to annoy and provoke them, especially when the marches go through Catholic areas. Catholics have tried to stop the marchers going through areas where they live. Crowds of Catholics sometimes gather by the route of the marches.

Look at Sources A, B, and C, which were taken in Portadown in 1996 and 1997.

A Portadown 1996. Panic and fear spread among Catholic protestors as the RUC make a baton charge to clear the road so that the Orangemen can take part in their traditional march.

 B

A Catholic woman, and Orangemen about to march along the Garvaghy Road, a Catholic area of Portadown, 1996. The original caption went on, 'about 300 Catholics attacked the RUC as they shielded the Orange marchers'. Can you see the armoured vans in the background?

1. Look at Sources A and B. These two photographs were taken on the same day, but we do not know which was taken first. Explain which you think was taken first and give reasons for your choice.
2. Look at Source B. What is the woman doing? How are the marchers reacting to her?
3. Can you see evidence in Source A to support the statement in the original caption of Source B?
4. Look at Source C. What evidence can you see of the heavy security?
5. What are the similarities and differences between the events shown in Sources A, B, and C?
6. According to the information in this feature alone, is it possible to say whether the police were guilty of taking sides?
7. Write an imaginary dialogue between the woman in Source B and the man at the front of the march she is talking to. Try to include as many ideas as possible from each side of the argument about the marches.

C 6 July 1997. Portadown Orangemen march along the Catholic Garvaghy Road. Heavy security was provided by the army and the RUC.

However, on 20 July 1997, the IRA announced another cease-fire. The political situation had changed in 1997. The Labour Party had been swept into power by a landslide victory in the General Election; and the support of the Ulster Unionists was not needed by the new Government. Gerry Adams and Martin McGuinness were also elected to Westminster as Sinn Fein MPs, but refused to take their seats as they would not take the oath of loyalty to the Queen. Mo Mowlam, the Labour Secretary of State for Northern Ireland, assured Sinn Fein that they would be allowed in to all-party talks if the IRA did establish a cease-fire. More importantly, she said that decommissioning would not become an obstacle at the beginning of negotiations.

The Ulster Unionists, led by David Trimble, said they would attend the talks. Unsurprisingly, the Democratic Unionist Party, led by Ian Paisley, declined the invitation to attend. The first meeting was held on 15 September 1997. Both the 'Official' Ulster Unionists and Sinn Fein attended the meeting. The two parties did not meet in the same room, but were at least in the same building! However, when Tony Blair went to Northern Ireland and met Gerry Adams in October, the Unionists felt betrayed when it was revealed that they had shaken hands (see Source A on page 4).

In November 1997, some senior members of Sinn Fein and the IRA decided to leave their organisations. A new group, led by the sister of the IRA hunger striker Bobby Sands, emerged, pledged to defend the ideal of a united Ireland. Then, on 10 December an IRA prisoner escaped from the Maze Prison. The following day, Gerry Adams went inside 10 Downing Street for talks with Prime Minister Blair. He was the first Republican leader to do so since Michael Collins met David Lloyd George in 1921. However, the rollercoaster of peace talks and violence continued. Two days after Adams met with Blair, there were riots on the streets of Derry, triggered by the Protestant Apprentice Boys' marches.

At Christmas 1997, a leading Loyalist prisoner, Billy Wright, was murdered by Republicans from the INLA (see page 34) inside the Maze Prison. In retaliation, Seamus Dillon, an ex-IRA member, was killed; and, on New Year's Eve, Loyalist gunmen shot five men in a Catholic pub. Then, on 5 January 1998, Loyalist prisoners from the UDA and UFF in the Maze Prison declared that they no longer supported the Stormont peace talks, because they felt that the British Government was making too many concessions to the Republicans. In an unprecedented move, on 9 January, Mo Mowlam went to the Maze Prison to meet the Loyalist prisoners, and was able to persuade them to continue supporting the peace talks, which restarted on 12 January.

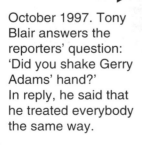

October 1997. Tony Blair answers the reporters' question: 'Did you shake Gerry Adams' hand?' In reply, he said that he treated everybody the same way.

David Trimble

◀ David Trimble (middle), with fellow Ulster Unionists Ken Maginnis (left) and John Taylor (right), arriving at Downing Street to have talks with Prime Minister Tony Blair, July 1997

▼ Leader of the Ulster Unionist Party
▼ MP in Westminster Parliament
▼ In 1997 he attended talks along with Sinn Fein, but refused to speak to them

When David Trimble became leader of the 'Official' Ulster Unionist Party, many people believed that he would adopt a more conciliatory approach. However, his condemnations of Sinn Fein and of Gerry Adams did not support this.

For a time in the summer of 1997, it looked as though his party would boycott the peace talks organised by the British at Stormont. Eventually, however, Trimble was able to persuade his MPs that talking, even with Sinn Fein representatives, was the best way forward.

However, he ruled out the possibility of talking directly to Gerry Adams and Sinn Fein. In December 1997, he predicted that the IRA would break its cease-fire during 1998.

Mr Trimble is the most significant figure in the search for peace. He must bear the great responsibility that is on him at this time.

Edward Kennedy, an American Senator, speaking in December 1997.

Gerry Adams

 Gerry Adams in Portadown, July 1997

In his youth Gerry Adams was a member of the IRA. Later he became active in Sinn Fein; and for a while was banned from speaking on British television under the *Prevention of Terrorism Act.* In the late 1980s and early 1990s, Adams held secret talks with John Hume of the SDLP (see pages 57 and 59), and visited President Clinton in the USA. He was important in bringing about the IRA cease-fire of 1994. Adams was elected to the British Parliament in 1997 with fellow Sinn Fein leader, Martin McGuinness. However, both refused to take their seats in the House of Commons. Later in 1997, Gerry Adams took part in the Stormont talks organised by the new Labour Government.

Adams has always said that he has influence, but no direct control, over the activities of the IRA. Some people, for example Ian Paisley, have never accepted this statement.

▼ Leader of Sinn Fein
▼ Elected MP in the British Parliament, 1997
▼ Negotiated with British Government and some Ulster Unionists in 1997 to try to achieve a peaceful settlement in Northern Ireland
▼ Invited to 10 Downing Street in December 1997 for talks with Tony Blair

E

Those who condemn the armed struggle have a responsibility to spell out the alternative course by which Irish independence can be secured. I, for one, would be pleased to consider such an alternative.

Gerry Adams, speaking in 1983 in reply to a challenge issued by the Catholic Bishop Cahal Daly. Daly had challenged Sinn Fein to look to peaceful ways of making progress.

A

Catholics stand in silence as an Orange march passes through their district

B

The ordinary Ulsterman is not going to surrender to the IRA or be betrayed into a united Ireland or put his neck under the jackboot of Catholicism.

Ian Paisley, 1982.

C

History says, Don't hope
On this side of the grave
But then, once in a lifetime
The longed for tidal wave
Of justice can rise up,
And hope and history rhyme.

So hope for a great sea-change
On the far side of revenge.
Believe that a further shore
Is reachable from here.
Believe in miracles
And cures and healing wells.

An extract from Seamus Heaney's poem 'The cure at Troy' 1990.

1 Look carefully at the expressions of the people in Source A. Explain as fully as you can what you think is going through their minds. You could choose just one of the crowd if this helps.

2 Explain why many Northern Irish Protestants might agree with the statement by Ian Paisley in Source B?

3 Study the poem, Source C. What hope do you think there is for lasting peace in Northern Ireland?

1921 London negotiations

1922 Treaty

Peace movements and progress through non-violent means

A An IRA bomb in Coventry, August 1939

B An IRA bomb at Canary Wharf, London in February 1996

Change and continuity (Sources A & B). The IRA bomb Britain 1939-1996.

1951, Orangemen march to celebrate the Protestant victory at the Battle of the Boyne **C**

Violent and militant action

1922-1923 The Irish Civil War

1916 The Easter Rising

1919-1921 The Irish War of Independence

1939 IRA organise a bombing campaign in mainland Britain

1956 IRA organises a new bombing campaign in Northern Ireland

1968 Civil Rights Movement

1970 The formation of the SDLP and Parliamentary Nationalism

1972 Direct rule from London introduced

1974 Power-sharing lasted from January to May
1974 General Strike brought about resignation of Brian Falkener and the end of power-sharing

1985 Anglo-Irish Accord

1994 IRA cease-fire

1997 IRA cease-fire

1997 Peace talks held at Stormont. Both Sinn Fein and some Ulster Unionists present. Sinn Fein leaders meet Tony Blair at Downing Street

PEACE

D Catholic Civil Rights marchers in Derry, 1969

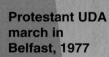

Protestant UDA march in Belfast, 1977 **E**

Similarity and difference (Sources C, D & E). Marching through the times.

1968 Outbreak of 'the Troubles' and British soldiers sent to Northern Ireland

1972 Bloody Sunday

1979 Assassinations of Lord Mountbatten and Airey Neave, MP

1981 Hunger Strikes

1996 Canary Wharf and Manchester bombs break the IRA cease-fire

VIOLENCE

*U*pdates

*U*pdates

Index